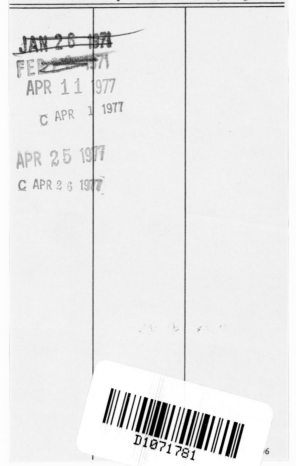

# THE CURTIS AFFAIR

## MARTIN S. ACKERMAN

NASH PUBLISHING
LOS ANGELES

*To those individuals
who remained my friends
during the troubled
times at Curtis*

Library of Congress Catalog Card Number: 74-118022
Standard Book Number: 8402-1133-3

Published simultaneously in the United States and
Canada by NASH PUBLISHING, 9255 Sunset Boulevard, Los
Angeles, California 90069.

Current printing (last digit):
10 9 8 7 6 5 4 3 2 1

Printed in the United States of America

# CONTENTS

# INTRODUCTION

This book, in the main, is self-explanatory. It represents my tenure at Curtis, what I tried to do, and why I tried to do it. I have thought long and hard about why a book of this kind should be written. Sometimes, it is best to leave things alone. However, so much has been written about Curtis, so many distortions have appeared in print, that I felt it necessary to more or less tell my side of "The Curtis Affair."

Most of what has been written, as you will discover in reading this book, is simply not the truth.

First, people have a tendency to exaggerate in order to
make a story interesting. Second, most of the writers
who have attempted an analysis of Curtis have had
their own personal ax to grind, one way or another.
The people who have written about Curtis, so far, have
been mainly former editors who have written about the
survival of *The Post*. In this book, I will try to give some
insight into Curtis' near-disastrous financial condition,
and our efforts to save the company from constantly
impending bankruptcy. While *The Post* did die, The
Curtis Publishing Company is still very much alive; *Holiday* is still alive, *Ladies' Home Journal* is still alive, and
apparently the company is in good enough shape to give
the Curtis trustees the hope of selling the company and
reviving its publishing activities. All creditors have been
paid, and the disaster of bankruptcy has been avoided.
The key, to my way of thinking, is that not only are all
the magazines still publishing, but that most of the employees have their jobs—many with different employers,
but they are, nevertheless, still employed and working
on the magazines which were once part of the great
Curtis empire.

Undoubtedly, the question of *The Post*'s
survival represents failure—failure because I thought
it could be made profitable and could be kept open.
I was wrong. And if it could not be made to pay,
then it had to close. Was the try worth it? I still
believe so, although I have probably as many scars
as anyone from "The Curtis Affair." My basic

philosophy in life has been to try, even if it's
very difficult, because that's what life is all about.

Why did I get involved in Curtis? Sincerely and
forthrightly, I thought it represented an outstanding
opportunity to put Perfect Film & Chemical Corporation further into the publishing and subscription
business. We had entered the publishing business
through the acquisition of *Popular Library* and
*Magazine Management*. We were now ready for
more, with some big league magazines and the
largest circulation company in America. The tax
loss and the value of the fixed assets looked doubly
attractive in view of the fact that we had used all of
our loss carry-over at Perfect and could liquidate the
fixed assets into net worth. The deal looked attractive,
especially since we could get involved without the
chance of any financial loss. What I failed to see
was that Curtis was like a big fishbowl, and that
nothing could be done without major headlines. It
is impossible to reorganize under those conditions.
The newspapers and magazines anticipate your every
move, and make it impossible to make the kind of
liquidations and changes that have to be made.
The biggest mistake I made was giving out the
first interview; I should have known better.
At the time, it looked like the right thing to do. As
one gets older, one learns—and I certainly have
learned.

# CHAPTER ONE

# A SPECIAL MEETING

*"A special meeting of the Board of Directors of The Curtis Publishing Company was held at 2:00 p.m. on Monday, April 22, 1968. Present were . . ."*

Minutes of board meeting

# 1

Confrontation is a strong, restless word. In the frantic, frustrating search for a new way of life, youth is pitted against age, new ideas against the status quo, black against white, and everything against everything. That is the common concept of matters relating to the word.

Seldom, however, do we hear reports about upheavals and confrontations taking place in the world of business. Yet those of us who have had opportunities to look behind the closed doors of corporate

boardrooms have had our eyes opened again and again.
We see top executives locked in struggles of great bitterness and intensity, generating shock waves that have
far-reaching consequences. Such infighting eventually
becomes of great significance to the public at large,
to the shareholders of the companies involved and, of
course, to the individuals caught up in the actions.

One of the great business confrontations of all
time took place on an otherwise ordinary Monday, in
March of 1968 in Philadelphia. The event was the
culmination of a series of events reaching far back
into American history; the implications of this event
will not fade from the scene for many years to come.
Certainly not for me!

On paper it was all very simple. A special meeting of the Board of Directors of The Curtis Publishing Company was held at 2:00 p.m. on Monday,
April 22, 1968. Present were eleven men—all outstanding businessmen—some of whom had served
Curtis for a long period of time, others of whom had
just become directors. It was certainly a "Blue Rib-
bon" group, by any standards. Only two members
were absent—Ellsworth Bunker and P. A. Sugg.

The first order of business was simple. The
Curtis Building, owned by the publishing company
and located in Independence Square in Philadelphia,
would be sold for $7.3 million. The transaction was
just one in the series of sales of the valuable assets

of Curtis which were being made to keep the company alive.

J. M. Clifford, then president of Curtis, reported a proposal which I had made under which Perfect Film & Chemical Corporation, which I headed, would arrange for a $5 million loan to Curtis. This loan was to be secured and guaranteed, and would give Perfect Film a chance to see whether the combinations of the activities of the two corporations made any sense. The proposal was discussed at length, along with a number of alternate proposals for obtaining the immediate capital needed by the company. Later in the afternoon, Milton Gould, a director, told the Board that I had informed him that the Perfect proposal was subject to withdrawal if not accepted then and there at the meeting. Accompanied by former governor Alfred Driscoll, another director, I was invited to attend the board meeting for about twenty minutes.

After further discussion, my proposal was approved and I was elected a regular director, along with Eugene Mason, Perfect's attorney. Clifford was voted out of the presidency of Curtis and elected chairman of the Board of Directors. I was made president in his place.

This was no usual board meeting. It was a crucial step to try to salvage the tottering Curtis Publishing Company. Of perhaps greater interest to the American public, it was also an attempt to save *The Saturday*

*Evening Post*, one of the nation's most venerable insti-
tutions, from dying of a long and lingering disease.

I was a key figure, and at the same time, a
highly controversial one. I was an outsider—according
to some, "a brash young thirty-six-year-old entrepreneur"—an upstart who had all but forced himself into
a kind of elite, closed business "club," whose members
were, for the most part, conservative old-line Phila-
delphians. According to my critics, I seemed an
unlikely candidate for the position. My family and
friends could not understand why I needed this kind
of job at all.

Even though I was not in at the start of the
board meeting and had but a few rushed minutes
to get acquainted, my very definite impression was
that those present resembled men groping along
unfamiliar passages in the dark. They seemed to be
fumbling with a number of slippery alternatives to
their severe financial crisis without ever really being
able to grasp and hold any feasible solution. Years
of what one observer called a "forget-it-and-it-will-
go-away" attitude had brought Curtis management
to a sad state indeed.

All the directors knew the facts, but only a few
would face up to them.

At one point, the depressing meeting recessed
while Clifford and another board member, Moreau
Brown, telephoned The First National Bank of Boston,

the company's principal creditor. Immediately thereafter, they reported to the Board that the bank had
agreed to carry the debt that Curtis owed for two
more weeks while alternate proposals to the Perfect
Film & Chemical plan were sought and reviewed. Upon
being questioned by the directors, the bank had also
assured them of my own credit and integrity.

The meeting dragged on and on, interminably,
while I awaited the outcome in a nearby executive
conference room. At about three-thirty, three directors
left the boardroom—Gould, Brown, and Driscoll.

They asked me if I would wait two weeks to
give the Board and President Clifford an opportunity
to consider the Perfect proposal or to find some other
solution. My answer was, "No. It's now or never."
They would either have to accept Perfect and its
money at once, or Perfect's interest in Curtis would
come to an immediate end.

Governor Driscoll invited me to discuss the offer
with the entire Board. Present in the oak-panelled
boardroom of Curtis, seated around one of the most
formidable directors' tables imaginable, were Cary Bok,
Moreau D. Brown, J. M. Clifford, Alfred S. Driscoll,
Walter S. Franklin, Milton S. Gould, Thomas J. Hyland,
Lawrence Kessel, G. B. McCombs, and Robert D.
Patterson. Also present were Allison Page of the firm
of Pepper, Hamilton & Scheetz; Donald Ziegler of the
firm of Price Waterhouse & Co., auditors for the

company; and Miss Gloria L. Swett, secretary of the
company, who was recording the minutes of the meeting. I made my presentation—simple and direct—to the
Board. In my opinion, I said, Curtis was in real financial trouble. The company needed immediate action.
The injection of new money was, of course, urgently
required. But I pointed out that this was really second-
ary to the greater need: the application of strong,
sound management techniques, so long lacking in the
company. That, I said, should be the first order of
business, rather than an endless round of shopping for
money.

No one could really make an intelligent appraisal
of Curtis Publishing, and its future, until in-depth
studies had been made of the affairs of the company—
where it had been and where it was going. With the
help of Perfect, I was certain that such an appraisal
could be made, and made fast. Then the Board of
Directors would be in a reasonably good position to
know what direction could be taken. A merger with
Perfect, for example, was a possibility.

I informed the Board that it was necessary for
Perfect to obtain the consent of The Fidelity Bank of
Philadelphia for the arrangement of the loan to the
publishing company under Curtis's basic bank loan
agreement. We had secured such consent and felt that
with the assistance of Fidelity, The First National Bank
of Boston, and the Board of Directors of Curtis, at

least the immediate financial crisis could be staved off.
I held out no promises of blue skies; rather, I was
critical about what I knew had to be done. At 4:30 I
left the meeting.

The minutes of the April 22, 1968, meeting state
that Mr. Thomas J. Hyland made a motion that was
seconded by Mr. Lawrence Kessel, and that all members present voted in favor of the Perfect proposal
except Messrs. Bok, Clifford, Driscoll, and Patterson,
all of whom abstained. I was elected president and
chief executive officer. Clifford was elected to the post
of chairman of the Board. Mason and I were asked to
rejoin the meeting at five o'clock.

The minutes, however, were not recorded exactly
as the events occurred. Cary Bok, it has been related
by a director who was present, though abstaining at
first, tried to change his vote to no the following day.

After I got into Curtis, it became quite clear to
me that the company was not in a strong enough
position to become a merger partner for Perfect Film
& Chemical Corporation or, for that matter, anyone
else. The best that could be hoped for was that the
company would avoid bankruptcy and create a shell
of a company with cash or certain liquid assets, and
a large, fresh, tax-loss carry forward. This corporate
vehicle could then be built into something.

At that time, I did not plan to be the person
who would completely rebuild the vehicle. Surely

someone else could be found to take over this challeng-
ing task. Rather, I thought that once the company was
in fairly good shape financially, I would leave and
devote my time to Perfect and to the operational arms
of this vehicle.

I visualized Curtis as three separate companies.
First, the parent, The Curtis Publishing Company,
would become a *holding company*. This was necessary
because of its problems under the preferred stock indenture which made it impossible for Curtis to borrow
any money for longer than twelve months. It seemed
to me that this provision could be changed once we
had something to offer the preferred shareholders.
But first of all, Curtis would have to be put into a
cash position in order for it to become an attractive
acquirer and buyer of other companies.

The second part of the company was to be the
magazine arm. I believed that *The Saturday Evening
Post* and *Holiday*, along with *Status*, which we were
to acquire later, could become the nucleus of a new
publishing company and constitute the beginning of
a vital new publishing concept. By cutting *The Post*
back to three million readers and *Holiday* to one
million readers, and holding *Status* to one hundred
thousand, I saw the possibility of creating a quality
network of magazines. The new *Post* would cater to
subscribers from the upper side of the demographic
scale, with incomes of $10,000 and above, 80 percent

of whom seemed to live in the so-called A and B counties. These were the people—the ones with standing and
good incomes—that advertisers wanted to reach.

Look had tried this approach quite successfully
with its so-called Top Spot, wherein it sold separately,
at premium prices, the best quality one million names
on its list. Advertisers were convinced that these were
the people they needed—the spenders who could
afford the goods and services advertised and who were
not being reached effectively by television.

To my mind The Saturday Evening Post, unlike
Life or Look, was a reading, rather than a picture
magazine, and therefore should be directed towards
an affluent, better-educated audience, which had the
time, intelligence, and inclination to appreciate quality
fiction and articles. The Post had an enviable reputation among readers, if not among advertisers.

Moreover, by producing a three million-circula-
tion product, there would be less pressure for a
couple of years to go after extra subscribers—a costly
process. Holding tight could mean a substantial saving,
in the millions. I also hoped that the cutback in circulation would upgrade The Post's image, with everyone
clamoring to be among the magic three million. Thus, in
time, we might even be able to get some full-priced subscriptions sold, in addition to achieving better newsstand
circulation. Perhaps the idea might catch the imagination
of the advertisers and their agencies.

In any event, it would give our salespeople something different to sell. They would not be competing
directly with *Life* and *Look*, but could turn to the
advertisers who were now placing their advertisements
in news magazines like *Time* and *Newsweek*, and other
class-type magazines. It seemed like a sufficiently
unusual, though realistic, plan to give us some hope.

Steve Kelly, the publisher of *The Post*, was instrumental in the execution of this concept. He did a great
job in selling the image and the reasons behind the
change on the presidential level to the advertising
agencies. After all, the alternatives were pretty dismal:
either to close the magazine down, or to stay in competition with *Life* and *Look* and continue, like them,
to lose advertising pages.

Economically, the cutback meant that we had
three million fewer magazines to lose money on—a
fact which could reduce our break-even to manage-
able levels. And advertisers who could not afford to
buy the large books like *Life* and *Look*, might find
their way into the new-class *Post*.

*The Saturday Evening Post* needed a bold move
supported by new-risk money. Ten million dollars of
new money was later to be put into a newly formed
Saturday Evening Post Company, along with the $5
million and three magazines from Curtis. With enough
decisive moves, The Saturday Evening Post Company
could become an effective publishing force. Curtis

could either keep its $10 million investment intact or
sell it off and have funds to move itself forward. Of
course there were problems, but the way things looked
as we progressed, the plan had a good chance of
succeeding.

# CHAPTER TWO

# "HELLO, MR. GOULD,..."

*"Hello, Mr. Gould, I don't know if you remember me, but my name is Martin Ackerman. . . ."*

Telephone conversation
March 2, 1968

# 2

There are many, many talents, varying from those in art and music and the theater to growing prize marigolds, winning at bridge, and bringing up children. Much rarer and less celebrated, but still very much a "talent," is the one for making sick companies healthier. This, it seemed from experience, was my gift; or so I thought at the time this whole incredible story began in the spring of 1968.

Thinking back, I guess this awareness of a talent already proven was why I, the "brash young entrepreneur," could try to tell a group of distinguished executives how to run their business. It did not discourage me that I was only thirty-six, while these older men had a combined total of more than one hundred years of experience in magazine publishing. How else can I explain what to an outside observer must have seemed like sheer nerve—or, as others have called it, sheer ego?

Even as a boy, growing up in Rochester, New York, I seemed to get involved in saving things and in trying to chart new paths through the forest that were better than the established ones. I remember well that when I first arrived in New York City in 1957, my ambitions were to get heavily involved. I was fascinated by corporations and the way they worked. And I constantly wondered why managements operated—or perhaps failed to operate—in a particular manner.

After graduating from Rutgers Law School near the top of my class, I clerked for a period with an outstanding appellate judge, Milton Conford, from New Jersey. My first position after passing the bar was with the firm of Phillips, Nizer, Benjamin, Krim & Ballon, at a time when "Louis Nizer" was a household phrase.

But I was a young man in a hurry, and I felt I wasn't moving ahead fast enough. In less than a year I left to join Rubin & Rubin, a law firm specializing in

corporate acquisitions, security regulations, and proxy
battles. Here I learned so much so fast that by 1961
I felt ready to launch into my own practice as a specialist in the field of preparing complex stock registration
statements for other lawyers. I enjoyed being "a lawyer's lawyer"; and both financially and professionally
I did very well indeed.

In 1962 I became a senior partner in a labor law
firm with the specific goal of setting up a corporate
securities department. But the timing was wrong. A
slump in securities registrations followed the June,
1962, break in the stock market. Clients were scarce,
and I didn't have the time or patience to sit around
waiting for the economic climate to improve. Instead,
I decided to leave the active practice of law to go into
corporate investment and management.

Scouting around for a company in need of
help, I found an excellent candidate in Perfect
Photo, Inc., a company with a scattered network
of small photo-finishing operations. Although the
corporation enjoyed sales to the respectable tune
of $21.2 million, it had earned only $401,000 in
1962. I was certainly no professional when it came
to experience in the photo-finishing business. But
I had concentrated with such absorption on management strengths and weaknesses that I was certain
that I could come to the aid of Perfect, no matter
what its field of operations.

In November, 1962, along with some associates whom I had interested in the venture, I bought 300,000 shares of Perfect. This represented a 21 percent interest in the company and, more importantly, working control.

I began by establishing some cost controls which, though they helped the earnings picture, were not enough to wipe out the dismal balance sheet, needless debts, and a lot of intangible assets that were not good enough to permit me to borrow the money with which to make sound acquisitions. There seemed to be no internal solution to our problems, so I looked outside and found a likely target—United Whelan Corporation, a shrinking  ugstore chain with a Tiffany balance sheet.

After a great deal of infighting, maneuvering, and debating, I finally gained control of Whelan. The first thing I did was sell off the money-losing discount and department store operations. With the proceeds I bought control of a vitamin company and an importer of plastic products. Seemingly an ungaily combination, it was actually remarkably workable. With the acquisitions consolidated under the new name, Perfect Film & Chemical Corporation, we were in business—a *healthy* business.

By the time I started negotiating with Curtis, Perfect was doing a solid business of about $100 million, with earnings of about $4 million, or $2.75 a share. I had also continued to buy new operations and

sell off marginal ones. Certainly I wasn't always right
in my evaluations, but to my way of thinking, if I
could prove right 60 percent of the time, I would end
up a winner.

When Curtis fell in line on the cross hairs of my
sights, it impressed me as the biggest and sickest com-
pany I had ever seen, but nevertheless still salvageable.
Standard & Poor's Corporation in the Standard Listed
Stock Reports of February 14, 1968, said of Curtis
Publishing:

> Based on a projected improvement
> in the economy, revenues for 1968 are ex-
> pected to top those of 1967. . . . After a
> slow start, operating results for 1968 may
> improve from those of 1967.

The "long term" prognosis was that "Prospects
will be significantly influenced by the success of *The
Saturday Evening Post* in increasing advertising revenue
and by the company's ability to acquire profitable
terms."

Although as late as 1960 Curtis had enjoyed an
annual revenue of $260.5 million, with an operating
profit of $9 million, by the time I had entered the
picture that figure had dwindled to $124.6 million,
with a staggering loss of $62 million.

Curtis's equity in just six years had shrunk

some $40 million—to $16,854,000, according to its
annual report of 1967. This loss came in spite of the
fact that, in 1965, Curtis received a $24-million wind-
fall by selling its mineral rights in Canada. In other
words, some $54 million of stockholders' assets went
down the drain under the faltering management of
the Curtis trustees. As I shall mention again later
in more detail, it was estimated that some $34 mil-
lion alone had been lost in trying to keep *The Saturday Evening Post* alive.

    This was the depressing picture Curtis presented
when on March 2, 1968, I placed an important telephone call to a man whom I had once met only briefly.
He was the director mentioned in Chapter 1, Milton
S. Gould, a prominent lawyer. Gould was considered
the *"enfant terrible"* of Curtis, a thorn in the side
of the trustees for some years past. During the 1930s,
he had been a federal prosecutor, and many of the
attributes of the prosecutor persisted in his forensic
style. His principal reputation had been gained in
complex corporate and securities litigation. Gould was
an eloquent speaker, and a kind of unofficial historian
of the company. The trustees positively disliked him,
while other directors, particularly Brown, Franklin, and
Patterson, seemed to have high respect for his abilities
and knowledge. To me, he was to become a man who
could neither avoid a battle nor abandon a friend. Why
he had stuck it out through all the past and current
agitation, with little or no reward for his efforts, is

understandable. Gould had come to Curtis as a representative of his clients. When they sold their stock, he stayed
on for two reasons: (1) he regarded it as a kind of public duty, and (2) he was asked to remain by some of
the other directors.

This was the kind of man who, though I little
knew it at the time, I was phoning on that fateful day
in March, 1968.

"Hello, Mr. Gould," I said, "I don't know if you
remember me, but my name is Martin Ackerman, and I
was involved in Pathé Industries, Inc. I wonder if I
could come over and talk to you about The Curtis Publishing Company. I know you're a director, and I thought
I might have some ideas on how to help the company in
its present difficulties."

Gould's response was hardly encouraging. Right off
the bat he told me I was wasting my time, not to mention his. The situation was too tough for anyone to handle
and besides, there was nothing to talk about until the com-
pletion of an important meeting to be held in Boston on
Saturday, March 30. When I persisted, he finally con-
sented to meet with me in his office on Monday, April
1, at 5:00 p.m. Just before he hung up, however, he
again assured me that I was wasting my time.

In the meantime, other things that I would soon
learn about were happening at Curtis. Toward the end
of 1967, Curtis' lead bank, The First National Bank of
Boston, had advised Milton Gould and Moreau D. Brown,
a partner in the banking firm of Brown Brothers

Harriman & Co., that they were dissatisfied with Curtis management. The bank said that they no longer trusted Curtis president John M. Clifford and his people; they thought (quite rightly) that facts had been concealed from the directors and that Brown and Gould were the strongest men on the Board. The bank felt that they had no choice but to call their loans, a step that would throw Curtis into immediate bankruptcy. Although Brown and Gould understood the bank's position only too well, they were convinced that the imminent crisis could be staved off with the sale of the Curtis headquarters within the period of the bank's extension.

But the fact of the matter was that the March 30 meeting Gould had mentioned to me had been called because the sale of the building was *not* going to take place within the bank's grace period. The bank, upon learning this, again politely but firmly warned Gould, Brown and Clifford that, if Curtis management were not replaced, the loans would be called.

On April 1, 1968, I met Milton Gould at his office and immediately outlined my plan to save Curtis. I told him that if the Curtis Board of Directors would accept the offer, Perfect Film & Chemical Corporation would (with the permission of its banker, The Fidelity Bank of Philadelphia) lend Curtis the sum of $5 million on an equal basis with the bank loans now owed. In return, I expected a place on the Board as well as the position of chief executive officer. Once inside Curtis, I would see whether the company was a candidate for a merger with Perfect. Or,

if not, I would recommend to the Board a plan to keep
the company out of bankruptcy.

A month had passed since our telephone conversation, but in that time Gould's skepticism seemed, if
anything, to have increased. He insisted that the job was
too big for me or anyone else. "In any event," he pointed
out, "it's not up to me but to the banks, in particular
The First National Bank of Boston, and the Curtis Board.
The person you really ought to see is Mac Clifford."

The following morning I was ushered into the
office of J. M. Clifford, President of the Curtis Publishing Company. Again, I came right to the point. If
Curtis' problem was money and management, Perfect
Film and I could help on both fronts. Unlike Gould,
Clifford's response was based on optimism; he did not
feel that Curtis really needed any help, or any outside
help. Curtis was, he said, in fine shape. It was true
that funds were a bit tight right now, but once Curtis
had survived the normal summer slump it would make
a profit for the year. The problem was merely a
temporary shortage of working capital; however, if I
wished, we could discuss the matter further after
lunch.

That noon, I lunched with Perfect's bankers in
Philadelphia. From them, I learned that Clifford, a
lawyer who had once been a vice-president at NBC,
had been asking some questions that displayed more
than a passing interest:

"*Who* is Martin Ackerman?"

"*What* is Perfect Film & Chemical Corporation?"

The Curtis situation derived from financial matters both archaic and complex. Working control of the company traditionally lay in the hands of the Cyrus H. K. Curtis Trust and the Curtis heirs. Cyrus Curtis had left his controlling stock in trust with this provision: "Believing that the success of The Curtis Publishing Company will be promoted and best insured by the continuance, as far as possible, of the present management and policy, it is my wish and I direct that during the continuance of this trust, my common stock of The Curtis Publishing Company shall be retained by my trustees and shall not be sold unless some extraordinary contingency shall arise making it desirable to sell, and then only in the event that my trustees unanimously agree."

The Trust was to continue through the lives of his daughter and her son, and over the years the Board of Trustees has been composed of the immediate heirs, including Mrs. Mary Curtis Zimbalist, daughter of the Curtis founder, and her son, Cary Bok. The Trust holds 17.3 percent of the outstanding Curtis stock; another 14.7 percent is in the hands of their heirs, totaling control of 32 percent of the company.

Thus, the impact that the members of the Curtis family exerted upon the destiny of the company far exceeded their numbers. Cary Bok was the treasurer and senior vice-president. Yet he acquired the name of Curtis' "invisible man" because he spent most of his time in his native Maine. A company plane was maintained, in

fact, largely for the purpose of flying Bok to Curtis board
meetings held the same day as the trustees meetings.

So much of the current misunderstanding of the
Curtis predicament can be traced to the *Annual Report
to Shareholders* for the year ending December 31, 1967,
and dated March 29, 1968. According to this report, on
December 31, 1967, Curtis was in default on its bank
loans and therefore insolvent, and the banks had given
Curtis an extension until March 31, 1968, to clear things
up. The condition was clear enough, however, to the
sophisticated analyst who read the footnotes to the
financial statements and made a few simple calculations
in the balance sheet.

(Gould reported later that the default in the loan
agreement was not disclosed to the Curtis Board of Directors. It came to the attention of Brown and Gould at the
meeting in Boston, when they saw for the first time the
annual report which had been mailed to stockholders.)

Curtis' working capital was short of the loan requirements and the current ratio was less than required.
But the true financial problem, and one that all of the
directors and I soon discovered, was an understatement
of Curtis' real liabilities by $60 million. In a liquidation
of the Curtis magazines, the company would have to
pay out $90 million worth of magazines to satisfy its
subscribers. The liability according to "generally accepted
accounting principles" for "unearned subscription
revenues, less related commission expenses" was stated
as only $31,172,000 as of December 31, 1967.

The company's last prospectus in October, 1967, stated: "The company's subscription lists represent a major asset in which the company has a substantial investment. In connection therewith, it had at June 31, 1967, unearned subscription revenues, less related commission expense, of approximately $31 million. The company had previously expensed approximately $13 million of costs, other than related commission expense, incurred in obtaining the unfulfilled subscription open at June 30, 1967. These costs, if reported under an acceptable alternative accounting method employed by certain other major publishing companies listed on the New York Stock Exchange and the American Stock Exchange, would have been recorded as deferred assets. The deferred asset of approximately $13 million would have been deducted from unearned subscription revenues in the company's financial statements at June 30, 1967, increasing the stockholders' equity by a like amount."

Incredible! A liability is an asset, but maybe it's a liability — in my opinion a $90 million liability rather than a $31 million one! The stockholders' equity in the December 31, 1967, report would have to be adjusted from $16,584,000 to a loss of $60,060,000. It also seems clear to me now that in spite of all efforts to sell the various Curtis magazines and the rumored estimates of their great value, no deal had ever been made before I came to Curtis because

nobody, including the present Curtis directors, ever
understood the actual effect of this liability upon the
affairs of Curtis and its chance of survival.

# CHAPTER THREE

# ANY MOVE IS A MOVE AHEAD

*"If you get gun-shy and are
afraid to be wrong, you can't
move a company ahead."*

Martin S. Ackerman, quoted in
*The Wall Street Journal*

# 3

One of my predecessors at Curtis made this remark, shortly after he had given up the seemingly impossible task of reorganization: "I often felt as though I were trying to put together the world's most complex jigsaw puzzle, with half of the pieces missing."

I am not sure whether I have quoted him exactly, but this was the general idea. As he went on to say, whenever there was nothing specific or real to fill some information gap, you could always find someone who would give an opinion off the top of his head or make a forecast. The recent history of Curtis is a jigsaw puzzle of formless and ever-changing forecasts, compilations of "constructive" suggestions or Jeremiah-like prophecies of doom. Everyone wanted to get into the act, and any basis that struck the forecaster's fancy seemed to serve the purpose.

One such forecast was in the form of a memorandum to J. M. Clifford from K. B. Artz, dated April 3, 1968: "The profit and loss forecast for the year 1968 now indicates a loss from operations of $1.3 million as contrasted with a break-even in the previous forecast. This results primarily from a reduction in the number of advertising pages we estimate will be sold for *The Post* and *Holiday* and a loss of income due to lower subscription and newsstand sales for the year."

Artz went on to say that the forecast was based on an anticipated 900 pages of advertising in *The Post*, adding that this estimate "appears to be somewhat optimistic." He wound up the forecast with the far from optimistic prediction that "if the sales of advertising pages for *The Post* do not improve, our loss would be somewhat greater than $1 million for the year."

Serious studies of the Curtis financial picture made at the time I took over the company underlined the fact that with every passing day the magazines were losing more and more money. Shutting down the magazines seemed the only solution, but

there would still remain the baffling question of what
to do with the $90 million-worth of magazines owed
to subscribers. To make matters worse, most of the
subscribers' $90 million went for sales commissions and
the cost of mail solicitation. Curtis operated on the
theory it was best to incur the obligation to its readers
and then rely on the advertisers to provide the money
for fulfillment. However, with the rapid decline of
*Post* advertising pages, this obligation took on the
dimensions of a nightmare.

*Forecast 1968 Operations for Board of Directors
Meeting,* more popularly known as the "blue book,"
came into my hands at my first meeting with Clifford
and his auditors. An impressive document prepared
each month by the company's accounting office, it
sought to show a cash forecast as well as the profit
and loss for the month of the total company, *The
Post, Ladies' Home Journal, Holiday, American Home,
Jack and Jill,* the circulation and subscription companies, plus a forecast for the balance of the year. As
one director observed, "The report was impressive,
except that it was always wrong. The forecasts were
never met."

The report for the April 4, 1968, meeting showed
an anticipated loss of the year ending December 31,
1968, of $1 million against a loss in 1967 of
$4,839,000. What was more important to my analysis
was the fact that if you added back the depreciation

and depletion, the company had forecast a "cash
profit" for the year ending December 31, 1968, of
$1,943,000 against a cash loss of $692,000 for 1967.
In any event, if you believed management, as I had
little reason not to in April of 1968, "the picture," as
Mr. Clifford had put it, "is not so bad."

On April 4, the Curtis Board of Directors met.
Recommended were two new directors, Thomas
Hyland and Lawrence Kessel, both of whom had made
fortunes doctoring sick companies. Hyland, former
*Time* editor and soft-sell business man, had been the
man who helped restore the Philadelphia & Reading
Company to health, while the Harvard-educated
Kessell had, as he said, "never lost a patient yet."
These two and their associates were looking for a
Curtis turn-around, and wanted to be on the inside
when it happened. How much real cash they had
invested in Curtis is hard to say, but they did represent
large stockholdings.

Tom Hyland and Larry Kessel worked in concert.
Both were diligent workers, strong, and generous with
their time and ideas. They attended all meetings and
were to make significant contributions. Both Hyland
and Kessel believed, as I did, that The Curtis Publishing Company could achieve success as a valuable corporation, if perhaps in a different structure than its
current one.

At the April 4th meeting, Clifford reported that
the sale of the headquarters building, although
approved by the Board of Directors on February 1,
had not been consummated, and it now seemed unlikely that a purchaser would be found. He also reviewed
the meeting at The First National Bank of Boston
which had taken place the preceding Saturday, and
informed the Board that the bank had extended its
loan until April 30.

Whether or not all the Board members realized
the seriousness of the company's financial condition
at that time is difficult to say, since for some years
past the minutes of the Curtis' Board of Directors
meetings have been of the short-form type, reporting
the resolutions but not the underlying discussion
or reasons.

On Monday, April 8, at 10:00 a.m. I met with
William Thompson and Peter Read of The First National Bank of Boston in the bank's sparsely furnished
conference room at 67 Milk Street. I sketched in the
background of Perfect Film & Chemical Corporation,
leading up to October of '62 when Perfect went into business of salvaging sick companies in which no one else was
interested. I then explained the unique system of management which the company had subsequently evolved.

With a management heavily oriented towards
strong division managers, both the management service

staff and I were free to work on problems with other
companies offering Perfect long-term growth opportunities. Having gained entry into publishing through the
acquisition of *Popular Library* in 1965, Perfect now
felt that photofinishing and publishing meshed very
neatly within the framework of a service industry in
the leisure-time fields.

Thompson's main concern seemed to be how
Curtis would obtain the $5 million which, according
to the company's management, was necessary to tide
them through the summer. He also warned me that,
since Curtis management usually understated the
financial statements, the problems were actually worse
than they seemed. I explained my plan to lend Curtis
the requisite amount immediately, in which event we
would rank on a *pari passu* (equal, without preference)
basis with the bank. This would give us a chance to
review the company's operations and recommend to
the Board ways in which Curtis might be saved from
bankruptcy. I also told Thompson that I felt that
our experience selling drug stores in New York City
back in '65 would help us in unloading unprofitable
divisions of Curtis as well as in making other appropriate rearrangements of the assets.

Initially Thompson balked at the fact that Perfect's $5 million would rank on an equal basis with
the banks, of which The First National Bank of Boston
was the leader. I explained that Perfect's bank, Fidelity,

would not allow Perfect to get involved in this situation
unless they were convinced that Perfect wouldn't lose
money in the deal—and in the light of my preliminary
view of Curtis' assets, I felt I could convince them
of this.

I was then introduced to Charles Moore, a senior
vice-president of The First National Bank of Boston,
who had taken over from Serge Semenenko the hand-
ling of the Curtis loan.

Semenenko, senior vice-president of The First
National Bank of Boston, is one of the leading corporate finance men of the generation. In the course of
some three decades Semenenko had arranged more
than $5 billion in loans for his bank, none of which
had gone sour. This financial genius had first come
into the Curtis picture back in 1963 when the company was embroiled in similar financial troubles. In
a desperate search for someone who could figure out
how to lend Curtis long-term money and still be
protected in the event of liquidation, Joe Culligan
is generally credited with finding Semenenko. Thompson and Moore expressed the hope that Curtis
wouldn't go sour either, so that Semenenko's record,
spanning the period from the mid '30s to the '60s
(he had now left the bank), would remain unblem-
ished.

Semenenko's plan, which he hoped would
satisfy the preferred shareholders, was this: Instead

of eliminating the debt restrictions entirely, the debt
limitation would be left intact while permitting specific borrowings of $35 million of which $22 million
went to exchange the short-term loans owed by Curtis
for five and seven-year notes and another $8.5 mil-
lion for a similar exchange with respect to the New
York & Pennsylvania Co. Inc., Curtis' paper-making
subsidiary. The remaining $4.5 million was put into
the bank as revolving credit for working capital back
in 1963. Management was also authorized to borrow
another $5 million through 1970 subject to the bank's
approval. The deal was sweetened by payments of
$3.00 of the arrearages owed to the $4.60 preferred
shareholders, and $0.60 to the $1.60 preferred shareholders. The shareholders overwhelmingly approved the
loan agreement, which is embodied in the basic bank
agreement dated December 17, 1963.

Thompson pointed out that, if Perfect wanted
to rank equally under the basic bank agreement, the
company could not immediately loan Curtis $5 mil-
lion; instead, the maximum amount that could be
safely loaned was $2.5 million.

However, with the sale of the Curtis Building, it
was anticipated that by June an additional $3.1 million
could be made available to Curtis. Thompson also
informed me that The First National Bank of Boston's
partners, Franklin National Bank and the Bank of the
Southwest, would have to be consulted before any
agreement could be reached.

This basic loan agreement became the underlying
and key document in all financial deals with Curtis
from April, 1968, on—a fact which very few people
fully understood.

It was lawyer Peter Coogan of the eminent
Boston firm of Ropes & Gray who elucidated the
complications of the December 17, 1963, basic loan
agreement, and who pointed out that all rights to
borrow under it would expire December 31, 1968.
Obviously, if anything was going to be accomplished,
it would have to be done between April and December.
The general concensus seemed to be that, considering
the critical financial condition Curtis was in, the
preferred shareholders would never agree to any extension of modification of the basic loan agreement
which would ultimately jeopardize their values in
liquidation.

We agreed that further discussion should be
had with Gould to see if he could get the Board to
support the proposal. An appointment was made for
me to see Gould at his office the next morning,
Tuesday, April 9. Having brought in his law partner,
Bernard Fischman, an expert in financial and corporate
transactions, Gould seemed more inclined to discuss
what could be done with Curtis.

He defined two major problems. First of all,
Curtis, having been on the brink of bankruptcy so
long, did not really appreciate the seriousness of its
plight, and Gould felt it would take a real shock to

the system to sell any proposal to the Board of Directors at this time. Clifford especially was sure to prove antagonistic. Having survived the Culligan, Clay, Blair, Marvin Kantor era, along with numerous other threats to his authority, Clifford was anxious to retain the company presidency. According to Gould, the key figure in this presentation would be Moreau D. ("Doc") Brown who was the link between the old members of the Board, Cary Bok, and the bankers at The First National Bank of Boston.

Second, it was imperative that we convince The First National Bank of Boston of the soundness of our proposal since without their complete support there was no chance of any deal between Perfect and Curtis. Gould questioned whether Brown would accept Ackerman and Perfect but, having been there so long, trying so hard, he would try once again. The link between Brown, Perfect, and the Philadelphia segment of the Curtis Board might be Perfect's bank, The Fidelity Bank.

Gould agreed to accompany me to a one o'clock meeting arranged for that day at the Carlyle Hotel. After a hurried call, Jim Johnston, a credit analyst for The Fidelity Bank, also agreed to be present, along with Bill Thompson. E. Eugene Mason, a Philadelphia lawyer and, to my mind, one of the finest legal minds in the country, also attended.

Once more the program was presented and the financial condition of Curtis reviewed. Based on

information supplied by Clifford and Gould, it
appeared, superficially at least, that the immediate
major problems were working capital and stemming
what looked like moderate losses for the year. Though
the job seemed simple, in fact it was not. All of the
bases upon which decisions were made proved to be
inaccurate, and the financial condition of Curtis was
really far more critical than anyone could have
imagined.

The senior officers at The Fidelity Bank set up
a meeting between Doc Brown and me on the eleventh
in order that I might explain my plans to him. Brown
listened well but said little. He asked Fidelity if it was
prepared to help me if such help were needed, and
whether or not it would give Perfect permission to
lend Curtis the requisite $5 million. A senior vice-
president of Fidelity said, in effect, that if Ackerman
asks us to do it, we will, because in all our dealings with
him since '62 he has kept every promise he has ever
made, and I see no reason to believe he wouldn't keep
them this time.

On Monday, April 15, a meeting was held at the
offices of Oppenheimer & Co., Perfect's investment
bankers, at which the Curtis proposal was once again
outlined. The partners of Oppenheimer questioned why
Perfect should be interested in lending Curtis $5 million.
The answer: This was an opportunity—an opportunity
similar to the one Perfect Photo had taken advantage
of in 1965 when they got involved with United

Whelan—an opportunity similar to other opportunities
Perfect Film had seized since October of '62—an opportunity to get inside Curtis, to make a loan that could
be secured, and to examine the company to see what,
if anything, could be done, and finally to make a
proposal. The bankers got the message. If Curtis failed,
from the image point of view, the failure would be
enormous; if successful, this transaction and the potential of the ultimate combination of Curtis and Perfect
could catapult Perfect into a major American company.
If the risk seemed great, then so too did the potential
for gain.

During this period, Curtis had retained White, Weld
& Co., and Loeb, Rhoades & Co., to try to find a
financial solution by way of merger or otherwise. Milton
Gould insisted that before he would take the responsibility of sponsoring my proposal, he wanted White, Weld
and Loeb, Rhoades to look me over, discuss the matter
with me, and confirm that they had no better alternative.
Accordingly, Gould arranged to meet at the offices of
Loeb, Rhoades a day or two before the Executive Committee meeting in Philadelphia. Present at this conference,
which took place in John Loeb's office even though he
himself did not attend, were representatives of White,
Weld and Loeb, Rhoades, and the situation was
discussed. Gene Woodfin of Loeb, Rhoades summed it
all up at the end of the meeting by conceding that
since the Loeb, Rhoades-White, Weld combination had
no solution of its own to offer, it came down to the

proposition that it is "either Ackerman or bankruptcy for Curtis."

On Wednesday the seventeenth Clifford called an Executive Committee Meeting of Curtis at 10:00 a.m. to consider Perfect's proposal. Prior to this, I discussed with Clifford the chances of the proposal's acceptance. A noncommital man, Clifford only replied that he thought the situation wasn't as severe as Gould and the banks had made out; there were numerous other proposals pending before the Board and the Executive Committee; and that as far as he himself was concerned, he hadn't really made up his mind as to what he would recommend.

Meeting promptly at ten, the Executive Committee invited me to present my proposal at about eleven. As it now stood, my plan was simple enough: Perfect would lend Curtis $5 million under the basic loan agreement of December 17, 1963; I would be elected president and chief executive officer of Curtis; E. Eugene Mason would join me on the Curtis Board and be elected secretary; I would serve without compensation for an indefinite term at the pleasure of the Curtis Board of Directors; Perfect would be paid for its services in a manner agreed upon by the Board. It was a hectic meeting, at the conclusion of which the Executive Committee agreed to recommend me to the Board of Directors and in general, to accept the Perfect offer.

# CHAPTER FOUR

# THE PROBLEM OF POSITIVE THINKING

*"Ackerman Seeks 'Positive Plan'
for Curtis but Denies He Intends
to Fold the Post."*

*The Wall Street Journal*
April 24, 1968

# 4

I t has often been said, in numerous ways, that a
man who is critically ill and sees death not far
away will take almost any kind of quack medicine
suggested, in the hope that it may effect a cure. When
I first arrived at Curtis the "medicine" the corporate
patient could not get out of his mind was the sale of
the Curtis Building. The trustees all seemed to feel
that once this was consummated, the company would
automatically emerge from the ill health of red ink
and into the black.

On April 23, 1968, the Board sent out a news
release announcing its plans to sell the company headquarters building for $7.3 million. This sale would, it
was felt, bring in enough much-needed cash to relieve
Curtis of its financial inflammation. This move, which
was definitely not my doing, provoked a barrage of
rumors—like almost every other move anyone was to
make at Curtis. The sale was interpreted as a prepara-
tory step to moving corporate headquarters away from
Philadelphia. Since the fact of the matter was that the
deal involved a lease-back arrangement whereby the
company would retain use of some 50 percent of
the building, we actually entertained no thoughts at
all of relocating.

The very fact that we were selling off property
so quickly led to speculations that I was also planning to lop off *The Post*. The truth of the matter was
that no one wanted any more desperately than I to
see the magazine restored to its former illustrious
position. Clifford's emphatic statement to the press
that "We absolutely, positively, and unequivocally are
not planning to suspend publication of *The Saturday
Evening Post. Period*" typified the kind of protesta-
tions we were forced to make. But the more we pro-
tested, the thicker and faster the rumors flew. To
make matters worse, *The Post* had been changed from
a weekly to a biweekly during the previous change of
chief executives in 1964, and, since making it a monthly

was hardly feasible, it was generally assumed that the next logical step would be total extinction. The debate eventually polarized into two camps: those who honestly believed that I wanted to save *The Post*, and those who vociferously supported me, not because they believed in my integrity but because they were afraid that any doubting-Thomas statements to the press would undermine the already shaky underpinnings of the Curtis structure.

The multitude of problems afflicting Curtis when I arrived on the scene could be boiled down to one major issue—leadership. Since the early '30s the company had been run according to an outmoded Main-Line Philadelphia philosophy, with the president, directors, officers, and most of the top executives hailing from the old school of management. Although they possessed managerial talents, experience, and skill in abundance, they had grown smug and complacent. The ups and downs of the company were, to their way of thinking, simply the vagaries of business fluctuation. There always would be a *Post*, a major star in the constellation of national magazines, as surely as there would always be a Main Line.

Certainly, from the early '30s to the '50s, when the advent of TV threatened other media, Curtis was indeed secure. A company which could advertise regularly in *The Saturday Evening Post* might congratulate itself that it had "arrived." When the first auto ad

appeared in the March, 1900 *Post*, the event marked
the beginning of a mutually beneficial relationship that
was to survive to the end.

The auto makers' loyalty to *The Post*, an enigma
to *Life* and *Look* executives, can be traced back to the
days of Horace Lorimer whose "relaxed" approach to
business subjects earned the magazine the reputation
among intellectuals as "America's largest trade journal."
Lorimer encouraged businessmen to tell their own
stories which, in a day when attacking the giants of
industry was *de rigueur*, had an obvious appeal to
executives.

*The Post* and the automobile industry rode a
smooth superhighway to success. Cyrus Curtis was
reported to have been earning $5 million a year in
the early 1920s, and Curtis' prosperity was shared by
the stockholders and company employees.

In hindsight, however, it is apparent that the seeds
of future trouble were being sown in the very heyday
of Curtis' affluence. Paradoxically, an abundance of
success and a failure at diversification early in the game
laid the groundwork for subsequent trouble.

Curtis was a businessman without any illusions
about his editorial skills, but he operated on the belief
that a first-rate magazine invariably had a first-rate
editor. After all, he reasoned, the success or failure of
any magazine ultimately depended upon its readership.
People either liked it and came back for more, or they

didn't. Any historical review of the company's peaks
and valleys bears out its founders' philosophy: periods
of prosperity can without exception be linked up with
the reigns of top-rate editors. Hugh Hefner's creation
of *Playboy* and Helen Gurley Brown's resurrection of
*Cosmopolitan* are two cases in point. Whatever their
detractors might say, Hefner and Mrs. Brown saw a
need and filled it, resulting in healthy magazines and
fat profits.

The profit and loss statements of the Curtis magazines during the tenures of Edward Bok and Lorimer
reflect their editorial acumen. Their magazines sold
heavily off the newsstands and raked in advertising
dollars.

In 1925 The Curtis Publishing Company ranked
as one of the most successful businesses in America,
earning $16 million after taxes. Nevertheless, great
financial risks were implicit in the situation. Cyrus
Curtis was seventy seven years old; if he were to die,
the members of the family would have to sell so much
of their common stock to pay inheritance taxes that
control of the company would be lost—a dilemma
faced by many family-controlled businesses today.

Working control of the company lay in the hands
of the Cyrus H. K. Curtis Trust and the Curtis heirs.
This was the way Cyrus Curtis himself had left his
controlling stock in trust. The directors were often in
a somewhat unbalanced position. In the early days,

the director's role had been associated with that of a
trustee. He was subjected to the same rigorous fidu-
ciary discipline in order to insure the performance of
his office solely in the interest of the corporation as
a beneficial trust: contracts between a director and
his corporation. Contracts between corporations having common directors were similarly condemned on
authority of trust precedents. From the beginning,
the trust analogy was not a happy one. Not only did
the obvious legal differences in the position of a
trustee and a director make it inept, but the director's
practical need for a great freedom of initiative made
the trustee's straitjacket a troublesome restraint.
Directors, unlike trustees, do not hold legal title to
the property entrusted to them. They act under a
general grant of authority to manage the business,
while a trustee is narrowly limited by the terms of
the trust instrument. A simple majority of the directors may bind the corporation, whereas trustee
action must be unanimous.

The Curtis preferred stock plan, which was the
device used to retain control with the Curtis heirs, was
complicated. But if one had faith in the unending success of the publishing company, this posed no real
problem. The company distributed some 700,000
shares of preferred stock valued at $100 a share to
the holders of the common stock, thereby giving the
preferred shareholders first call on future earnings of

the company with their dividends to be paid before a
penny was parcelled out to the common shareholders.
Further, the preferred stock indenture stipulated that
the holders were to be paid first in liquidation and
that the company was prohibited from making loans
beyond twelve months. It is important to bear in mind
that, at the time, it looked as though there would only
be profits and the company would never have to borrow to keep itself alive.

There is little doubt, to my way of thinking, that
this plan was the main reason why no one has ever
wanted Curtis for a merger. The creation of the preferred stock and its provisions against borrowing, along
with the liquidation terms, set the company's financial
tone for the rest of its life.

Recently, in addressing a management group at
the Wharton School of Finance in Philadelphia, I
remarked that there is a lesson to be learned from the
architect of the Curtis preferred plan, Mr. Francis
Scheetz of the firm of Pepper, Hamilton & Scheetz:
*Never let a company box itself into a position where
it loses its flexibility*! In business, today's successful
enterprise can be tomorrow's failure, and a business
which has achieved success in one enterprise can fail
in others.

This was the case with Curtis. Every effort the
company made towards diversification met with failure,
beginning with its seemingly logical attempt to enter

the newspaper business. The Curtis Publishing Company, which had such a running head start, soon found itself bypassed by lesser competitors who moved ahead through aggressive and imaginative acquisition programs. There is no reason to believe that Curtis should not have been first in book publishing, first in newspapers, and first in broadcasting. But once the company had tried and failed, it seemed as though management simply backed off any further attempts at building a broader base for future growth.

During the early days of the 1920s Curtis declared a monthly dividend, unlike most public companies which declared a dividend quarterly. However, the common shareholders received little between the 1930s and '50s, since the company was committed to paying the preferred shareholders first, originally to the tune of $6.3 million a year.

Cary W. Bok, as a trustee, was instrumental in having the preferred stock indenture amended to reduce the preferred shareholders' requirements, but nevertheless the main provisions with respect to borrowing and liquidation remained the same. Old-timers at Curtis credit Bok with this one contribution, but Bok didn't go far enough.

Profits evaporated so rapidly that by 1961 The Curtis Publishing Company found itself in serious financial difficulties. On March 29, 1962, Robert H. Mac-Neal, then president, announced for the first time since

the company's incorporation in 1891 that The Curtis
Publishing Company had sustained a loss of $4 million.

How could this have happened? To my mind,
Curtis had suffered from lack of real leadership since
its inception. The currents of change which were revo-
lutionizing the publishing world in the 1950s were too
strong for Cary W. Bok and the trustees of the estate
of Cyrus H. K. Curtis, and men like Walter Fuller and
Bob MacNeal. The Curtis company's failure was, essen-
tially, the failure to find bright new faces in management who could innovate and move with the times.

Cary Bok was treasurer of Curtis and a senior
vice-president, but he was the company's "invisible
man." Nobody ever saw him since most of his time
seemed to be spent hiding out in his native Maine.
Curtis, at great expense, operated an airplane for the
express purpose of flying Bok to Curtis board meetings. The only confrontation I ever had with him was
when I announced my plans to sell the company's new
King Air plane on the grounds it was an extravagance
Curtis could ill afford.

In the winter of '62 Bok had been in a Boston
hospital for major surgery. While recuperating at his
Maine retreat, he fell and broke his leg. Under Curtis'
bylaws, he was charged with presiding over board
meetings in the absence of his old friend, Robert A.
MacNeal. A phone call came the day before the meeting: "MacNeal is out of town. Should the Curtis plane

be sent up for you?"

"Hell, I'm flat on my back in bed," Bok told Philadelphia. "I resign as acting president. Work something out."

The directors' decision: fire MacNeal. Later, Bok observed, "It was obvious that MacNeal had to go."

Joe Culligan also had his problems with Cary Bok. After an initial era of good feeling in the spring of '64, Culligan was shocked to receive a memo from Bok describing in vivid detail the great hardship the Curtis-Bok family would undergo if the Curtis headquarters buildings, which for decades had supplied heat and power to the Bok family-owned Public Ledger Building, were sold.

Bok is also reported to have played a key role in disposing of Joe Culligan as president of Curtis. Bok allegedly encouraged editors Blair and Kantor to believe they could convince the Board and trustees to install Kantor as president. At the suggestion of one of Curtis's lawyers, Bok agreed to meet Kantor secretly, supposedly for the purpose of finding out whether or not Bok would support Kantor. Apparently, although Bok was courteous enough, he was actually backing J. M. Clifford as Culligan's successor. Kantor, along with Blair and Culligan, felt they had been misled by Bok.

This was the kind of leadership under which The Curtis Publishing Company was floundering!

On April 25, I achieved something of a victory as reported succinctly enough by *The Wall Street Journal:* NEW CURTIS PUBLISHING REGIME BACKED BY FORMER DISSIDENT. Philip P. Kalodner, the paper reported, had withdrawn his bid for the presidency of Curtis "for the time being," gallantly extending an "olive branch" to me in the belief that "new management is entitled to a fresh start." He actually did offer me his help and claimed he wouldn't seek a directorship at this time. At least for the moment, I was at the helm.

On April 24, 1968, the headlines in *The Wall Street Journal* announced: ACKERMAN SEEKS POSITIVE PLAN FOR CURTIS, BUT DENIES HE INTENDS TO FOLD *THE POST*.

A. Kent MacDougall, who wrote the story, quoted a spokesman for The First National Bank of Boston, to which Curtis owed $9 million, as commenting, "We view Mr. Ackerman's election as a constructive move. . . . We will work with Mr. Ackerman and the company (toward) hopefully a profitable future for Curtis."

Curtis, the article went on to say, was to have paid the four banks to which it was indebted about $9.2 million by March 31, but an extension beyond April 30 would now be no problem "in view of Mr. Ackerman's election and the pending sale of the headquarters building." Under the agreement with the banks, Curtis was required to maintain a working capital of at least $14 million from May to September and $18 million from October to April.

MacDougall reported the editors and executives of the various magazines were "favorably impressed with Mr. Ackerman's vigor and candor." Forecasts of "several insiders" suggested that John McLean Clifford, then sixty-three, would not remain as chairman much longer than his predecessor Culligan, who, after relinquishing the presidency in '64, stayed on as chairman for only four months before resigning.

Reports such as MacDougall's bolstered the public's confidence in the destiny of *The Post*, but as anyone in the limelight knows, the press also has its share of vultures waiting to leap at the slightest scent of corporate carrion.

Such a man is Bernard P. Gallagher, whose notorious *Gallagher Report* is the *Confidential* of the business world. Gallagher has a flair that approaches genius for crippling his victims, and the true extent of the damage he has effected by his malicious tactics, a mere fraction this side of libelous, can never really be estimated. Curtis was, of course, a Gallagher Gold Mine, and never did his talent for undermining public confidence in a company quite equal his defamatory attack entitled "The Curtis Story."

# CHAPTER FIVE

# A MULTITUDE OF PLANS

*"Curtis Publishing is a most curious company . . . it could . . . be the world's greatest headache or a glorious whaling voyage.*

Letter dated April 26, 1968

# 5

Not long after 1 moved into the thirty second-floor president's suite of the mid-Manhattan office building which housed Curtis' New York offices, I was deluged with as many and sundry plans for saving the company as I was with forecasts. And like the forecasts, some of these suggestions were extremely helpful; others less so.

One such analysis of the Curtis dilemma was sent to me on April 26 by Senior Editor Michael Mooney in the form of copies of two letters and three memoranda.

The first letter, written some time before to a British publisher in an effort to provide an historical overview of the company and a clarification of its operating problems, began: "Curtis Publishing is a most curious company. Depending upon your friend's taste for adventure it could appear to be the world's greatest headache or a glorious whaling voyage."

The letter then gave a rundown of the various Curtis magazines: *Jack and Jill* ("a quiet thing"); *Holiday* ("chugs along making a profit year after year"); *American Home* ("the handbook of style for the dreary lower middle class"); and *Ladies' Home Journal* ("John Mack Carter . . . has been successfully competing with his old friends at *McCall's*").

Then he came to Curtis' problem child, *The Post*: "If goodwill were cash, the beloved *Post* would be rich. But it's not. And the fortunes of Curtis depend a great deal upon the fortunes of *The Post*. . ."

Mooney proceeded to define the reasons, as he saw them, why *The Post* was losing money:

1. The great mass general interest magazines are in themselves "dinosaurs."

2. The growth of TV, "heady competition" from Time, Inc., and the growth of special-interest publications made *The Post* increasingly obsolete.

3. Just when every other publisher was

setting up many printing and distribution points, *The Post* was locked in the single, though huge, press facilities in Philadelphia.

4. Management and the old Philadelphia establishment were ignorant of the publishing business.

"Curtis," wrote Mooney, "has been sold more times than the Brooklyn Bridge." Although he was convinced that the company offered some sound assets as well as some "curious liabilities" to the buyer, the operational complexities were simply too much for anyone to cope with. He also came up with a good many ideas on ways to strengthen the editorial content of the magazine, labeling *The Post* "an inefficient carrier of national advertising."

Later, the editor of *Jack and Jill*, Karl K. Hoffman, pointed out that would-be advertisers lacked confidence in *The Post*'s likelihood of survival. In a memo to me he outlined an exceedingly unique plan to lure these reluctant advertisers back to the magazine:

My suggestion is quite simple, but it might be one that could be used during the next day or 120 days to reassure the advertisers and to hang on to the advertising dollars that we may lose because of the 'rumor factory' that is currently in operation. I suggest we offer advertisers double their money back if we

fail to publish the issue into which their
advertisement has been scheduled—and make
the offer valid for the next 120 days.

On the first of May, P. J. Kendall submitted his
suggestions for reorganizing and strengthening the Com-
mercial Printing Division, with the objective of increasing operational efficiency, reducing costs, and improving the profit structure.

First of all, complete facilities control should be
established, taking steps to assure joint responsibility
between the Manufacturing Division and the Commer-
cial Printing Division, including the sharing of personnel, setting of performance standards, and setting up
better cost control, scheduling and the purchasing of
new equipment.

Secondly, Kendall recommended that all Commer-
cial Printing Division personnel and functions be moved
to Sharon Hill in order to improve communications
and control, reduce duplication of effort, and make
possible on-the-spot checks of press, bindery, and
shipping facilities.

And finally, Kendall suggested that plate-making
personnel be placed under the direct control of the
division; that complete plate-making facilities be set up
at Sharon Hill; that unused or obsolete equipment, such
as a T-2 press, be sold; and that new bindery equipment, along with other more versatile and up-to-date
printing equipment, be acquired.

During that month of May, my desk was littered with similar suggestions and plans issuing from every corner of the company, as diverse and numerous as the spring flowers. And interestingly enough, like the spring flowers, they were the same old daisies that had reappeared year after year. Most of these ideas had already been submitted to my predecessors; and little, if anything, had been done about them.

Joe Culligan had labored long and hard to put innovative ideas into practice, but in the process he had managed to stir up too many hornets' nests at Curtis, and found himself constantly on the defensive. Defensiveness, in fact, was an intrinsic part of the Curtis environment.

And morale was low. During Culligan's tenure, company spirits had peaked. With his departure, they plummeted. The uncertainty of Curtis' future so affected personnel that many actually left; those who remained either did so out of a sense of loyalty or because they could not find better jobs elsewhere. It almost seemed as though the people at Curtis, from the top of the company hierarchy to the bottom, were suffering from some kind of economic battle fatigue.

W. E. Meyers, in a memo to Kenneth B. Artz, was one of a number of Curtis executives who underlined the severity of personnel problems. He wrote, "We should give immediate attention to employee morale and benefit programs. Some management decisions of the past six months, compounded by the public prognosis for the company and the communications gap which has existed during this period has endangered very seriously our retention of supervisory and middle-management people."

Meyers also recommended that a complete in-depth survey and evaluation of the data processing function be undertaken at the earliest possible date. The operation involved some $7 to $8 million, and was accused of employing a "patchwork, Band-Aid type of approach" utilizing computerization on a spot basis whenever a new crisis arose.

The whole cost-accounting system, he pointed out, needed modernization, with a complete revision of existing management-reporting requirements. Although the actual dollar saving of employee labor would not be very great, the improved system would be a kind of springboard whereby management might effect other economies.

Another innovative plan derived from Keystone Reader's Service, Inc., a Curtis subsidiary which had two major purposes: first, to make a profit (to be exact, $1,033,000 in 1967), and second, to obtain wide circulation for Curtis magazines.

Up until this time, J. T. Stewart of Keystone had opposed any proposals that *The Post* be discontinued. His reasons were self-evident: Keystone would be irreparably crippled if *The Post*—the Curtis leader at least in terms of reputation and seniority—were dropped.

But by now Stewart had changed his mind, realizing that losses of the kind *The Post* had been suffering would, if continued, ultimately topple the entire Curtis structure. He suggested instead that the company make an agreement with Time, Inc., to provide Keystone with increased quotas of a strong weekly magazine—such as *Life*—as a sales leader.

Stewart insisted that the time to act was now; my efforts to reassure Curtis personnel that decisive action would be taken, he said, had had a "dramatic effect" on company morale. The climate was right; the time propitious. Employee morale was once again on the upswing after a prolonged period in which personnel's tendency to let things ride—especially requests for salary increases—had made it not only difficult to hire competent people but to keep them.

Others also thought *The Post* should be buried. Director Noble Acuff was blunt in his statement of recommendation: "I would fold *The Saturday Evening Post* immediately. For the last several years it has continued to drop advertising lineage, in spite of the fact that the circulation has been increased and the latest Simmons Report gave us the best audience rating we have had."

According to Acuff, a deal might be worked out with Time, Inc, which would facilitate the continuation of some of Curtis' more profitable operations as well as improving profits. He felt certain that Curtis could secure *Life, Time, Fortune,* and *Sports Illustrated* for distribution, which would bring in an additional revenue of some $1 million for our Single Copy department. *Life* could serve a threefold purpose: It could be made available to the Curtis School Plan; Keystone Readers Service could be authorized to sell some 300,000 subscriptions per year; and finally, *Life* would provide our printing plant with the business needed to offset the loss of *The Post*. In such a manner, a competitor might be transformed into a savior, especially when a company is grappling with problems of such complexity that no internal means of solution can be found.

The company's paper mill, New York & Penn, was another Curtis headache for which a variety of nostrums were prescribed. H. C. Church estimated that somewhere between $50 and $60 million had been siphoned off this company alone within the past six years. "This company," Church observed, "has been bled white and it has no money left to pour into this endless chasm, wherever it is."

Difficult as it is to believe, New York & Penn was not even located in the proper geographic region to produce the kind of lightweight papers being used in competitive magazines, and the cost of shipping wood to the mill from regions where the right kind of trees did grow was prohibitive and economically unfeasible.

Equally untenable was the fact that all the paper machines of the Curtis mill were sized to the paper requirements of the company's present printing presses.

What would happen if publications desired to change their sizes to effect editorial improvements or to cut down on printing costs directly related to paper size?

Another fundamental problem was the small size and position of New York & Penn. During the past decade or so, while other paper companies expanded through acquisitions, mergers or heavy capitalization, the Curtis mill remained a midget among giants, surviving only by virtue of being a supplier to a captive market. Curtis thus found itself literally locked into a position that severely restricted design and editorial flexibility, so vital in magazines today.

One possible solution was to sell the mill to a large, well-established paper company which could convert New York & Penn into a plant producing a variety of papers. A transaction of this nature would doubtlessly require a commitment from Curtis to purchase its paper, at least for a stipulated period, from whatever company took over New York & Penn, but this disadvantage seemed minor compared with the current situation. However, even though the Curtis mill had been proposed for purchase to almost every large paper mill in the nation over the past couple of years, no positive steps had been taken.

Plans to improve the advertising picture also rolled in. "The name of the game is *money*," Mike Hueston wrote succinctly enough, adding, "and specifically, we must find a fast way to take in more than we pay out."

*Life* was charging $7.78 for every thousand people reached for a four-color page; *Look*, $7.16; *The Post*, a mere $6.39; and the *Journal*, an even punier $5.35. Even a small increase to $6.70 per thousand would have grossed about $2,000 more per four-color page in *The Post*.

Hueston was anxious to see Curtis explore every possible means of increasing advertising rates. It was a question of determining the proper cost figure that would give us more profit per page, even though we might end up with fewer gross dollars. He suggested that, through improved coordination and planning, quite a large chunk of the "down time" on Curtis presses could be used for jobs for Curtis advertisers. There were hundreds of potential ones around, but so far no one had made much of an effort to secure this kind of business.

Hueston concluded with a plan as intriguing as it was grandiose: "Why not turn the table and buy *McCall's* magazine. Combined with the *Journal*, it would be bigger than anything. . . ."

*The Post's* decline in advertising support was a major concern. The drop-off began in the early 1960s when the magazine began to fall out of step with the rapidly changing times, to lose touch with its readers. It looked as though *The Post* was in fact in danger of becoming a venerated anachronism. The first attempt to revitalize it failed, in my opinion, because, to go

along with Cyrus Curtis' tenent, the wrong editor had
been selected for the job. Clay Blair, for all his talents,
was too young and probably too much of a preacher.
With youthful enthusiasm, he used revolutionary
methods where evolutionary ones were needed. The
advertising people, naturally cautious about spending
other people's money, adopted a wait-and-see attitude;
and waiting, they didn't seem to like what they saw.
The new *Post* seemed a too drastic departure from the
old, especially in the face of increasingly stiff competition for advertising dollars from not only other magazines like *Life, Look,* and the *Reader's Digest,* but
from the increasingly formidable threat of television as
well.

Although *The Post* circulation at $7 million was
big, it was not the kind of circulation which captured
the interest of the advertisers. *The Post* was still by
and large a staple of small-town, middle-class America,
and the ad men were after the more affluent, sophisticated, "with it" urban population.

In the mid-fifties, *The Post* contained almost
1,500 advertising pages a year, and only 904 pages in
the last year of its life. Ad revenues, which stood near
$80 million in the 1950s fell to $41 million in 1967.
These statistics suggest the underlying reason why the
advertising community lost confidence in *The Post.*
Naturally, nobody wanted to see *The Post* die. As
Editor Mooney put it so well, "If goodwill were cash,

the beloved *Post* would be rich." But goodwill, especially to the advertisers, was certainly not cash. I was convinced that if the magazine was to survive, a *Post* success story would have to be written, and quickly.

The plan ultimately adopted provided for the setting up of a new company to be called The Saturday Evening Post Company which would be the primary publisher and owner of *Post, Holiday,* and *Status.* In this way *The Saturday Evening Post* could be revitalized with new capital funds, a separate identity and, most important, a new image which would attract the advertisers. This financial corporate restructuring, when combined with the editorial restructuring that had begun in May of '68, would give the magazine at least a fighting chance of survival.

Curtis was indeed a "curious" company. But whether from my point of view it was going to prove the vehicle for "the world's greatest headache or a glorious whaling voyage" remained to be seen.

# CHAPTER SIX

# "WHAT IS THE CURTIS PUBLISHING COMPANY?"

*"Curtis is one of the few publishing firms that starts with trees and ends up with magazines."*

Time magazine

# 6

The Curtis Publishing Company functioned under the outdated philosophy that the end products, the publications which people bought at the news-stands, arrived there *without being touched by any other human hands outside of the company.* The trees from which the paper pulp came belonged to the company. So did the logging equipment and the paper mills and the finishing plants and the printing machines —and all the people who operated them. The trustees

and the old employees were, in fact, intensely proud
of this purity and integration.

"Look," said one old-timer to me one day, waving
aloft a copy of *The Saturday Evening Post* and tearing
off a minute scrap, "every little shred of wood pulp in
this magazine came from Curtis forests, from trees cut
by Curtis men and processed in Curtis plants."

Yet what he—along with members of management
who should have known better—did not realize, was
that this very situation represented a tragic flaw in the
entire company's operations. At most magazine publishing houses, the loss of a page of advertising was
just that, and no more. But at Curtis, that loss rever-
berated right down into the roots of the company. It
meant lost time on a press, lost time in a paper mill,
a lesser need for pulp, and idle time for employees
all the way to the end of the line—the woodsman
felling the tree.

And any great fluctuation in advertising business
or in seasonal selling meant that the whole job-time
scale was continually moving up and down—a horren-
dous situation for managers in charge of employment,
trying to run efficient production lines.

"Duplication, inefficiency, and excess waste
abound." That was the way most Curtis executives
summed up the company operations. Possibly the
manufacturing aspects came in for a greater share of
criticism than, say, the less tangible ones like editorial.

But to someone coming into Curtis from the outside, this sense of overwhelming inefficacy ran like a scarlet thread through the entire company.

Costs were too high all across the board. The ratio of supervisors to hourly employees was much too high in many departments, especially in manufacturing. Elderly and infirm employees suffering from all manner of ailments were kept on year after year. Mailing lists, which might have been utilized to attract quick revenue at almost no cost through merchandising them to outside, noncompetitive firms, stagnated instead in musty file drawers. Inter-company communications were almost nonexistent, with divisions operating in isolation behind closed doors. Goals were seldom clarified; or if they were, only limited segments of the company were clued in to them. Employee morale was low.

The tragic irony was that the company had such rich veins of ore to mine. The book division, for instance, might have had enormous potential. Early in May, William Buckley reported that from 1965 through 1967 the division had produced some $9 million in gross revenues and generated more than $1 million in net profit for the corporation.

However, in recent months the profit curve had been dropping steadily and it looked as though it would continue to fall right through until the end of the usual summer slump. Early successes and the basic assumption that the base of six to seven million mail-sold subscribers would continue to buy books at the same rate (an assumption which turned out to be fallacious) contributed to the book division's too rapid expansion. The outlook for 1968 was bleak.

Buckley's analysis of the situation was that, since there were some two and a half million subscribers who were good prospects for Curtis books, even without any great expansion the division could generate "a handsome profit margin" on annual sales of $2 million or less. He recommended a revival of the all-time best seller *Audubon Nature Encyclopedia*, as well as several other popular Curtis series such as *Portraits of Greatness* and *The United States Encyclopedia of History*. By concentrating on sales in syndication, schools, libraries, and export markets, promotion expenses would be negligible.

A wealth of textual and visual material was gathering dust in the book division's files. It occurred to me that we could easily tap from this source editorial information rather than, as we had been doing, turning elsewhere for data on diverse subjects including food, health and travel. Time, Inc.'s increasingly successful book division had been born in the publisher's morgue where photographs and research material were stored. If Curtis, with a history going back to almost the eighteenth century, could not do the same with similar beneficial results, we deserved to lose our shirts.

Among the many recommendations for increasing company efficiency and profits was a memorandum from M. M. Schilbred sent to me on May 2. "Perhaps the most dramatic change that we could foresee," he wrote, "would be the change in dimension for the *Ladies' Home Journal, American Home, The Saturday Evening Post,* and *Holiday,* from their present size (680-line) to the more popular small size of 429-line."

The 680-line size was also used by some of our competitors, including *Life, Look,* and *McCall's.* The smaller size had been adopted by, among others, *Cosmopolitan, Good Housekeeping, Redbook, Family Circle,* and the *New Yorker.*

The economies to be derived from switching to the smaller size were considerable. A preliminary study comparing the production costs for the November, 1967, issue of *Ladies' Home Journal* with those of an issue in the smaller size indicated a cost reduction of approximately 30 percent (the figure stood at $2,450,000 versus $1,750,000). However, costs were based on using a similar number of pages, and there was some question as to how this would affect the amount and type of editorial content. More significant was the fact that the estimate for the smaller-size magazine was contingent on the use of *new* equipment. This brought us right back to the old problem of how Curtis could extricate itself from the straitjacket of its traditional arrangements.

A review of the circulation picture brought in this suggestion from C. E. Paperhausen: "Get out of the numbers game on Curtis magazines and go for a quality and more definitive audience obtained at a cost significantly lower than the income from said audience."

Paperhausen went on to observe that field-sold subscriptions (solicited by agents) returned almost nothing to the company in the way of income and produced an audience which failed to appeal to the advertisers.

He took issue with the severe price-cut offers, characteristic of past Curtis subscription programs, which tended to downgrade the apparent value of the magazines concerned. He further pointed out that these offers often antagonized newsstand buyers who resented shelling out the cover price for copies which could be otherwise purchased at about one-third of the price.

Paperhausen's recommendations included an impressive promotion campaign to build up the newsstand audience; continuing efforts to add new single-copy clients for Curtis Circulation Company and to pry some of the big ones away from present national distributors; and an all-out attempt to restore Curtis to a reliable shipping schedule, as late arrivals and irregular on-sale dates had damaged the reputation of all Curtis magazines at the newsstand level.

Curtis had the domestic and Canadian franchise, but no foreign rights, for Pocket Books. Paperhausen suggested that the company acquire the foreign distribution as well. He wound up his memo with a suggestion that was becoming all too obvious: "Lift the restricting cloud of bad personnel relations which we have been living with and which has badly damaged our employees' morale."

In an article entitled "New Man for Curtis" appearing in the May 3, 1968, issue, *Time* magazine quoted me as saying, after visiting Curtis's sales offices in California: "The employees seemed startled when I showed up. It was as though they hadn't seen anyone from Curtis in fifteen years." The communications gap between management and personnel was, to my mind, more a gulf than a gap.

The *Time* profile went on to report that I was either going to discontinue *The Post* or "remove it from competition with *Life* and *Look* by changing the circulation." "Curtis," I told the reporter, "is one of the few publishing firms that starts with trees and ends up with magazines. There is little flexibility among its divisions. . . ."

This was the Curtis dilemma when, in mid-May, I drafted an outline for the verbal report I was scheduled to deliver to the Board of Directors within a few days' time.

The report was an attempt to answer the
question: What is The Curtis Publishing Company? As
I visualized it, Curtis was really three companies in
one: the Manufacturing Division, with its printing
plant and paper mill; the Magazine Division, and its
various publications; and Circulation. Each division
was afflicted with its own debilitating disease.

In manufacturing, the fact that we could make
only a 42-pound paper for a 629-line page was a present flaw and a future impediment. In printing, we
were restricted to one size magazine.

A rundown of the magazines themselves indicated
that *The Post*, with its excessively "me-too" editorial
content, had lost the support of its advertisers. The
*Journal*, while it had excellent editorial content, was
too costly to produce and merchandise to compete in
the neck-and-neck fight with *McCall's*. *Holiday*, which
should have been a more generalized leisure-time
book, was hitting a too specialized market—the cost
per thousand was too high, the content too sophisticated, and the appeal was too oriented towards
women and older people. *American Home*, though
stable enough, lacked direction and had to be sold in
combination with other magazines. *Jack and Jill*'s
enormous potential had never been realized.

I strongly felt that all Curtis magazines should be
welded firmly into one strong demographic sell. In
this manner, the magazines would complement one

another and, together, present an attractive media
package for advertisers.

From the advertiser's point of view, *The Post*
could be the best magazine buy in the nation once it
was trimmed of the circulation fat and transformed
from a mass to a class magazine; it would be the
leader of the whole platoon of Curtis magazines. But
coordination was vital, not only in the overall, long-
run editorial planning, but also in reducing production
costs and wasted motion. Selling all the magazines as
a unit would also streamline the selling program. While
some advertisers, because of the nature of their products or services, would only want to appear in one or
two magazines, others would be interested in buying
the group, and what had been a single sale in the past
would become a multiple sale in the future.

Circulation was suffering from lack of leadership
and money. In order to compete successfully with
*Life, Look, The New Yorker,* and others, it should
have been moving with many other magazines and
books.

Subscriptions were weak. We were selling too
many "C" and "D" counties, and lagging in the more
affluent "A" and "B" ones. Direct mail was badly
handled. Strong continuing campaigns were needed to
boost circulation, instead of the present system of
selling by mail almost intermittently and then pushing
circulation to meet competitive increases.

All the nonprofitable divisions should be closed down, including the Book Division, the Audio Visual Division, and Curtis Enterprises, which handled special projects. The Fulfillment Center, which handled circulation, was another headache. Badly managed, it had cost $8 million and was adversely affecting the rest of Curtis's business.

Management in general lacked direction. Executives tended to work at cross purposes, and when confronted with a crisis, they either cut costs and/or people—rather like surgically removing the symptoms of a disease without even attempting to uncover and treat the disease itself.

Finally, my report focused in on the money problem. Curtis needed more money for the next twelve-month period if the company was going to move forward. Other company assets, of which there were many, needed to be realistically evaluated. For example, no one had really investigated the paper mill to decide whether it should be closed, sold, modernized or merged. From time to time someone would announce "The paper mill is losing money!" A flurry of activity would ensue, usually resulting in a quick, brief cost-cutting operation. This done, management would sigh with relief, relapse into apathy and wait for the next crisis.

Going right back to the pulp mills and the logging operations, one of the biggest problems at Curtis

was that management could not, to quote that long-
overworked saying, "see the forest for the trees."

# CHAPTER SEVEN

# THE IMPLICATIONS OF CHANGE

*"Sorry Mr. Rockefeller, You
Don't Quite Pass the Income
Standard."*

*The Wall Street Journal*
August 20, 1968

# 7

It was mentioned to me at one time that Curtis Publishing traditionally had been spending from 10 to 12 dollars for every subscription that came in for one of the magazines, with *The Saturday Evening Post* being at the high end of the scale. "If wishes were horses," I could wish nothing more, if this were true, than that just half that amount could be put back into the coffers for every subscription we intended to cut out under my new program. But I was not the only one who was agonizing over the past.

As for the future, the advertising fraternity was stunned by my announcement that we were going ahead with plans to slice the circulation of *The Post* in half. According to conventional wisdom, the only sensible way to salvage a sick magazine was to *increase* the circulation.

The move also provoked rumors that I intended to kill the magazine, not in one fell swoop but by degrees, lopping off bit by bit until there was nothing left. In an effort to squelch these rumors I assured Audrey Allen of *Advertising Age* that *The Post* still had, to my mind, a very important place in our publishing world. I pointed out that the percentage of *Saturday Evening Post* readers who also read *Life* and *Look* was probably less than twenty, suggesting that a substantial group of people wanted a magazine featuring in-depth articles about contemporary American society.

"There is," I said, "a great understanding of the people *The Post* serves. Outside sophisticated big-city areas, in places like Cleveland, Detroit, and St. Louis, skirts are getting shorter, people are catching up with big-city styles. Upper income families live there. The future *Post* will lead this group rather than what I think we have been doing—following."

An article in *Time* which caused waves in New York but hardly a ripple in my home town of Rochester quoted me as saying, "We tend to be influenced

by the environment we're in and forget the purchasing
power of the Rochester, New York, group. We have a
tendency to think that everyone lives and works in
New York, just because many of the editors and ad-
men do."

Asked about the threat of television, I replied
that I did not feel that *The Saturday Evening Post*
could compete with it, or, for that matter, should
even attempt to. Rather, we should find our niche in
terms of people served and assign a cost per thousand
to reach that niche. Once we had an improved, more
vendable product, we could become more aggressive.
Already Avis and Volkswagen were doing an outstanding job relying mainly on print to tell their story.
Ultimately the advertisers' love affair with television
would pale, and they would find their way back to
magazines.

I admitted, in response to questions about "efficiency moves," that we were taking definite steps, but
as far as I was concerned, cost-cutting was never more
than a temporary solution to the question of profits.
Sales, on the other hand, could cure a tremendous
number of ills. I assured the press that I could not—
indeed, would not—take any drastic steps without first
presenting the proposals and defining the reasons to
the Curtis Board of Directors.

On Friday morning, May 17, a special meeting of
the Board of Directors was held at the Curtis Building,

641 Lexington Avenue, New York City. Twelve of the
directors were present, with Cary Bok, as usual,
absent.

It was resolved that the Board endorse and adopt
in principle the plan for Curtis which I was presenting at the meeting. "Mr. Ackerman," said the minutes,
"reported that the large cash drain resulting from the
company's unprofitable operations had produced an
acute problem with regard to the operation of the
Curtis Circulation Company, that the client customers
of the Circulation Company were not being paid, and
that it looked as though the clients would leave, thus
rendering the company worthless."

The bad publicity generated by the publishing
company had seriously undermined the already waning
confidence in Circulation, and it was apparent that
this situation could not long continue without disas-
terous results. As I pointed out, it was even difficult
to ascertain the real earnings of the circulation and
subscription companies because of the manner in
which allocations of administrative and similar
expenses had been made among the corporation's various activities. Backed up by G. B. McCombs, I submitted the opinion that the subscription and circulation
activities *should* be able to produce at least $2 million
of pre-tax net income each year. Perfect Film &
Chemical would be willing to purchase the company's
business in these areas for whatever consideration

would be deemed fair by independent appraisal, provided that Curtis would guarantee that much earning over a period of ten years.

I proposed that the initial payment by Perfect be
$12.5 million in Perfect's convertible preferred stock,
which could be adjusted upward or downward in
accordance with the opinion of an independent
appraiser. The Board agreed, and it was settled that
Standard Research Consultants, Inc., a subsidiary of
Standard & Poor's Corporation, be engaged on behalf
of both Perfect and Curtis to determine the exact
purchase price.

In another step, agreement was reached on the
execution of the previously mentioned plan whereby
Time, Inc. and Curtis would jointly work toward
reduction of the circulation of *The Post*. Time had
already agreed to make available $5 million to Curtis
for working capital. This was on a basis similar to the
Perfect agreement.

"As a result of these two steps," I said later,
"Curtis can now concentrate on its magazine operations." That was as it should be. On May 17 we made
a joint announcement with *Time* that the plan had
been approved and that *The Post*'s circulation would
be reduced to about half its present size. *Life* was to
be offered to a substantial number of *Post* subscribers.

"Both magazines will be serving readers of equal
demographic excellence," I told the press. "Since our

arrangement with *Life* will result in our keeping a large number of those *Post* subscribers who also take *Life*, the quality audience of *The Post* is assured. They will obviously have the same upscale demographics that *Life* already has."

Jim Linen, president of Time, Inc., felt that these arrangements would be mutually beneficial. "Any growth in *Life* circulation resulting from these arrangements will be compatible with the magazine's current quality audience. Curtis will be able to reorganize on a more stable financial basis, and the magazine industry will certainly benefit from the presence of a vital and prosperous *Saturday Evening Post*."

The following day, the stock market report showed that trading had slackened. The Dow Jones industrial average was down 4.74, to 898.98. IBM had dropped, and Boeing was off 2 and 5/8. Curtis Publishing, however, was reported as the fifth most active stock, rising 1 and 7/8 points! It seemed like a good omen.

"We are going to get scrappy. And we are going to get lean," *Newsweek* quoted me. "At first glance," reported *Newsweek*, "Ackerman's scheme—to eliminate as much as half of *The Post*'s readership—seemed not only unproductive but self-defeating. But in the economics of the publishing business, the move had a certain logic."

Doubtlessly aware of its own cost and production problems, the magazine was quick to editorialize: "A large circulation does not always mean success. The formula for solvency is complicated, but one basic principle is this: as circulation goes up, so do production and distribution costs. Unfortunately, the extra revenue from rising newsstand and subscription sales doesn't always cover these costs. Profit or loss, therefore, becomes dependent upon advertising revenue."

Advertisers just aren't interested in the old numbers game. They want an audience of readers who are strong prospects for whatever the advertisers have to offer. Thus *Collier's* collapsed because, even though its circulation was 4.1 million, advertisers felt that the magazine was not really reaching buyers.

*The Wall Street Journal* applauded my deal with Time, Inc. as "a victory for Mr. Ackerman in his campaign to put Curtis back on its feet"; and *Business Week* hailed the event with headlines announcing a "New Bundle of Hope for Ailing *Post*."

"Industry observers think well of Ackerman and admit that the deal has a certain finesse," *Business Week* reported, adding, however, that the consensus of opinion was that Time, Inc. would probably get more out of the transaction than Curtis. In a nutshell, this was the arrangement:

*Time* would advance Curtis $5 million in working capital for an indefinite period.

*Life* Magazine would sign a printing contract with Curtis running until June 30,

1970, to help fill some of the production holes left by *The Post*'s diminished
circulation.

*Time* would throw its magazine subscription sales and distribution to Curtis'
profitable circulation subsidiaries.

In return for all this, *Life* would have
a quick, cheap way of pulling ahead of
*Look* in circulation. (The deal with *Life*
catapulted the magazine into the nation's
number one big-page spot, with a circulation of eight million, a fact that attracted
a lot of attention in the press and magazine
circles.)

*Business Week* predicted that advertisers would
flood the pages of *The Post* during the second half of
the year because, as of August 10, the ad rates would
be dropped from $27,585 per black-and-white page to
$12,780, in line with reduced circulation. Since *The
Post* could not strip away all of the expected circulation overnight, the magazine would actually be deliver-
ing about 4.5 million circulation for a great part of the
year. Thus, advertisers paying only for a delivery of
3 million would be getting a whopping bonus of
1.5 million!

Serious as the situation was, it was not without
humor. Journalists who found themselves removed from
the circulation lists lamented they had lost status and

could no longer face their neighbors. One columnist
reported that his wife was mortified to discover that *she*
had been cut off the list, while only a few days later,
*he* received an invitation to subscribe!

A *Wall Street Journal* headline quipped, "SORRY
MR. ROCKEFELLER, YOU DON'T PASS THE
INCOME STANDARD." Much to our embarrassment,
we had somehow managed to eliminate some VIP's in
the course of administrative surgery. The Rockefeller
concerned here was Winthrop who, residing in the rural
hinterlands of Arkansas, failed to pass muster. Also
eliminated were Mrs. William Kerby, wife of the president of Dow Jones & Co., publisher of the *The Wall
Street Journal* and, just to show no bias was intended,
Mrs. William A. Emerson, mother of *The Post*'s
editor.

Indeed, among the names eliminated was *my own.*
As *The Journal* explained, we were "victims of an
unfeeling computer that was ordered to knock out
70 percent of *The Post*'s rural subscribers and 50 percent of its metropolitan-suburban readership—and it
apparently went about the job without making nice
distinctions. . . ."

Art Buchwald turned the situation into an extremely funny dialogue which went in part:

> Feneker was at his law office in
> Hopskotch, Nebraska, when he received
> a call from his wife.

"There's a registered letter here from the Curtis Publishing Company," she said sobbing.

"What does it say?" Feneker asked.

"It says they're canceling our subscription to *The Saturday Evening Post*," his wife cried.

"But we've been subscribers for twenty five years," Feneker said.

"They mention that. They say we're too old for the magazine, and demographically we're unfit."

"There must be some mistake. I'll appeal it," Feneker said.

"The letter said the decision of the publishers is final. There isn't even a return address on the envelope."

Feneker started to panic. "Who knows about this?"

"I told mother. You were at lunch and I had to tell somebody."

"Good heavens. Call her right away and tell her not to tell a soul. If this thing gets out we'll be ruined."

Unfortunately, Feneker's mother-in-law had gone to a bridge game that afternoon and, as luck would have it, she mentioned it to her friends while she was the dummy.

Before long the phone started to

ring all over Hopscotch with the scanda-
lous news.

"They seemed like such nice people,"
Mrs. McMurdy said when her sister told her.

"I always thought something was fishy
when they drove around in a 1962 Ford,"
Chet McCauliffe told a friend when he
heard the news.

In a week's time Feneker started to
feel that his secret was out. No one came
right out and said they knew *The Saturday
Evening Post* had canceled his subscription,
but the atmosphere in the town had changed.

The bank refused him a loan on a new
wing for his house. He had trouble cash-
ing checks in the grocery store. The gas
station made some excuse why they
couldn't renew his credit card. He lost
the election for the school board and
there was even some talk that the bar
association would look into his
accreditation.

Lifelong clients took their business elsewhere. Mrs. Feneker was told
she was no longer needed in the car pool
for the children's dancing classes.

At school the kids were merciless
to the Feneker children.

One night Johnny Feneker came
home crying, his eye black. "They said

my father was a *Saturday Evening Post*
deadbeat," he said. "Say it isn't so, Dad."

"We're going to have to move from
Hopscotch," he told the family. "The dis-
grace is just too much to bear."

The *faux pas* resulting from our efforts to trans-
form *The Post* from a mass to a class magazine were
grist for Buchwald's comic mill, but sometimes fact
really *is* stranger than fiction. *The New Yorker's* "Talk
of the Town" reported, "A couple we know who live
on lower Fifth Avenue have had their egos lifted several notches by the discovery that, following *The
Saturday Evening Post's* computerized screening of
its circulation lists to winnow out undesirables, they
are now receiving two copies instead of one."

# CHAPTER EIGHT

# A MASSIVE ATTACK ON
# MASS CIRCULATION

*"Whatever the future has in store for The
Saturday Evening Post, issue 12A, used
in conjunction with the June 15th issue,
may become a primer for publication
designers. . . ."*

*Magazine Industry Newsletter*
*June 11, 1969*

CHAPTER EIGHT

A MASSIVE ATTACK ON
MASS CIRCULATION

# 8

Witty though some of the comments in the newspapers and magazines may have been about those who were unwittingly lopped off the circulation lists of *The Post*, the underlying causes were far from humorous. Here was prime evidence that Curtis methods of operation were highly questionable in many respects. My plan to cut circulation had been thought through with great care, and with a definite, and realistic, purpose. Yet when it was put into effect, little more was done than to punch some buttons on a computer that, to begin with, was not suited for the purpose. And the results certainly made *The Post* look ridiculous—especially to the advertising community that we were trying to reach with the greatest effectiveness.

Whether the press was greeting my moves and announcements with kudos or carping, there was at least this consolation: the adjectives used to describe my personality and style were invariably forceful. I was variously described as "fast-moving," a "wheeler-dealer," "decisive," and as having a "commanding style." Whether the adjectives were complimentary or pejorative was not the point. The image pleased me, not out of vanity, but because decisiveness was precisely what had been too long lacking at The Curtis Publishing Company. Years of ineffectual leadership had brought the company to its present predicament, and if I was going to accomplish anything, I had to "come on strong."

That summer Curtis was my major concern as we prepared to enter another phase in the development of the new *Post*. Philip H. Dougherty, advertising columnist for *The New York Times,* articulated our concept in his June 6 column:

> The first of the evolutionary issues leading up to the new *Saturday Evening Post* aimed at the class trade has just been run off the presses of The Curtis Publishing Company.

Only about 20,000 copies of the June
15 issue (out of a total circulation of 6.7
million) have the new look and none of
them is for sale. Most went to advertisers.

The "A Issue," as the people at the
magazine are calling the newcomer, shares
four articles and a fiction piece with the
regular run.

But the stories it doesn't share show
the new direction of *The Post*. They are
more highbrow. And some of the new
cartoons are more sophisticated. And the
type is bigger. And the layout has changed.
The cover logo is new, too, and Herb
Lubalin created it.

"For the editors, this step, then, is
a liberation. It means the freedom to
find and print the very best, from the
very best writers," says Martin S. Ackerman,
the new Curtis president, in an editorial in
A Issue.

Then, after describing the contents of the "new
*Post*"—an article by Clive Barnes on *Hair*, another on
John Kenneth Galbraith by John Skow, and still
another by William Saroyan—Dougherty continued:

In his editorial, Mr. Ackerman has a
thing or two to say about television—"twenty
years old, and it has generally failed to
improve"—and about the obsession of the big

magazines with the competition of television.

For *The Post,* he says there will be no more trick pieces to lure the throngs. "*The Post* will speak with a clean, sure voice to its natural readership, the cultivated Americans who want a quality of information and entertainment the mass media seldom provide—the people who like to have their intelligence honored, their opinions challenged, their personal worlds expanded."

*The Magazine Industry Newsletter* of June 11, edited by Leon Garry, saluted the "A Issue" with even greater enthusiasm:

Whatever the future has in store for *The Saturday Evening Post,* Issue 12A, used in conjunction with the June 15 issue, may become a primer for publication designers. Issue 12A is the first of the specially prepared "evolutionary" issues. The "feel" of the publication has been subtly altered by changing the cover stock to 110 pound from the usually variable 60 pound or 90 pound. The logo has been redesigned, preserving the "feel" of a tradition yet employing modern typography. The cover of 12A creates a George Wallace image; the standard June 15 issue's photograph has the impact of the 230th slide of a neighbor's

summer at Southampton. It would almost
appear that someone was striving to be
trite so that the "evolutionary" issue would
be a Hyperion to a satyr. Once inside the
book, one is immediately struck by the
changed layouts, the use of color, bold
face, and illustrations. The type faces
have been altered—larger and easier to
read, and no muddy sans-serifs to clog
the eye. Layouts are clean and color is
concentrated when used in conjunction
with bold face headlines to sharpen the
visual encounter or used boldly to balance illustration or typography. . . .

We then announced that starting with the September 7 issue the subscription price would jump more
than 50 percent from $3.95 to $8.00 or even more,
and that the newsstand price would also climb, though
only from $0.35 to $0.50. The price boost was an
effort to put things on a more realistic cost basis.

But just when the Curtis forecast seemed to be
clear and sunny, clouds from the past scurried into
view. On Tuesday, June 18, a jury awarded $1.8
million to former nightclub owner Lillian Reis in her
suit against *The Post* for libel and invasion of privacy.
Sensationalized by the press, it was the kind of case
that attracted wide public attention and consequently
dealt a lethal blow to our efforts to restore the magazine's image.

"They Call Me Tiger Lil" had been written five
years before, in 1963, by free-lance author Alfred C.
Aronowitz, at one time a pop music critic for *The New
York Times*. Apparently, Miss Reis put on the best act
of her life, breaking into tears when the verdict was
announced and, according to at least one newspaper
account, shaking hands with the seven men and five
women on the jury and embracing several of them.

I announced that we would appeal the verdict
immediately, and subsequently our attorneys came up
with some 115 reasons why their motions for a new
trial should be granted. But even if the verdict should
ultimately be reversed, the Tiger Lil case had already
proven an example of how the past can haunt the
present. The case, however, was only one such example.

In our efforts to reduce internal services and save
money, a company shake-up was mandatory. In order
to save $6 million annually, we had to let go some
450 employees, all of whom received severance pay
and compensation for accrued vacations. It was a solution we were loath to make, and one that provoked
widespread criticism; however, if the patient is certain
to die unless drastic surgery is immediately effected,
then the doctor has little choice. And at Curtis, the
death rattle could almost be heard.

Offsetting this was my decision on the same day,
July 3, to continue to operate the Sharon Hill, Pennsylvania, printing plant, which employed over two

thousand people. The printing plant had long been a
subject of debate. We had four alternatives: sell the
plant; lease it to an outside firm; close it down; or, as
I finally decided, continue operations as usual.

The Curtis Publishing Company's financial situation
was such a labyrinth that even the accountants could
not find their way out of it, as was evident in the
following extract from a letter I received on July 12
from our accountants, Price Waterhouse & Co.:

> We are unable to render an opinion on
> the combined financial statements of the
> circulation activities for the five years ended
> December 31, 1967, because of the substan-
> tial intercompany transactions between Curtis
> and its circulation subsidiaries which, in our
> opinion, were not conducted on an "arm's-
> length" basis. The arrangements between
> Curtis and its respective circulation subsid-
> iaries with respect to services performed and
> reimbursements therefore were to a great
> extent arbitrary. A substantial amount of
> general company overhead was charged to the
> subsidiaries without regard to specific ser-
> vices actually performed. Remittance rates
> and commission rates between Curtis and
> certain of its circulation subsidiaries were
> revised for various reasons from time to time
> at the direction of Curtis management. The
> financial data is not comparable over the

years because of the restructuring of the
circulation activities in 1966. Interest
expense on bank loans was absorbed by the
circulation company during periods when
the receivable from Curtis exceeded the
bank loans.

Immediately I wrote a long letter to Marvin
Chanko, treasurer of Perfect Film & Chemical, in
which I explained the accountants' inability to reach
an opinion, and attempted to define The Curtis Publishing Company's arrangements:

> For the years 1963 through 1965,
> Curtis Circulation Company performed
> not only the function of a sales organi-
> zation, which distributed the newsstand
> copies of the Curtis magazines and some
> 40 or so magazines and paperbound books
> for client publishers, and which solicited
> subscriptions through its school, telephone,
> and organization plans for the Curtis maga-
> zines and some 150 magazines for client
> publishers, but which also performed
> certain circulation planning functions for
> Curtis, although most publishing companies
> perform this function themselves. During
> this period, all direct mail, renewal mail,
> and agency business was also directed
> through the Curtis Circulation Company,

whereas publishers normally handle these
functions themselves.

During the years 1963 through 1965,
the Circulation Company was paid a commission of 11 percent on sales of the newsstand copies of the Curtis magazines
distributed by it, whereas the rates paid
by other client publishers were substantially less, ranging between 4 percent and 6
percent. Also, certain expenses incurred
by the Circulation Company on Curtis'
behalf were absorbed by the Circulation
Company, although similar type expenses
were reimbursed by client publishers.
During these years, Curtis Circulation
Company also received a commission
equivalent to 12½ percent of the price
of all subscription copies delivered to
the subscribers by The Curtis Publishing
Company without regard to whether or
not the subscription had, in fact, been
sold by the Circulation Company. On a
somewhat arbitrary basis, certain subscription expenses were reimbursed to
the Circulation Company by the publishing company while others were absorbed
by the Circulation Company.

In 1966, management decided that
the publisher should take over functions
previously performed by the Curtis

Circulation Company. Accordingly, a Director of Circulation was appointed in The Curtis Publishing Company and all publisher functions, including circulation planning, responsibility for direct and renewal mail efforts, agency business and related accounts receivable, etc., were transferred to The Curtis Publishing Company, leaving the Curtis Circulation Company as a sales organization distributing the newsstand sales of the Curtis and other publishers' magazines on a commission basis and selling subscriptions through its school, telephone and organization plans. The new commission rate established for Curtis newsstand sales for 1966 was 6 percent and remittance rates were established with respect to subscription sales for all Curtis magazines except *Jack and Jill* at rates of 5 percent for the telephone and organization plans and 10 percent for the school plan. A rate of 30 percent was established for *Jack and Jill* under all plans. Coincident with this reorganization, it was decided that the Circulation Company should be reimbursed field salaries as they related to newsstand distribution because circulation field personnel were presumably spending greater effort on the Curtis publications. There is some doubt as to the propriety of this arrangement in light of effort expended. In 1967, the

newsstand commission rate was arbitrarily
reduced to 4 percent and the remittance
rates to Curtis on subscription sales for all
magazines except *Jack and Jill* were changed
to 30 percent for the school plan and 10 percent for telephone and organization plans.
The remittance rates for *Jack and Jill* were
increased under all plans to 50 percent.

During the period 1963 through 1967,
The Curtis Publishing Company allocated a
significant amount of general company overhead to the Curtis Circulation Company as a
management fee. The amount charged to the
Circulation Company was based on a percentage of projected gross revenues. When the
reorganization was effected in 1966 (in the
latter part of the year retroactively to the
beginning of the year), no adjustment was
made to the intercompany overhead allocated
to circulation for 1966. Accordingly, in 1967,
a substantially smaller amount of general
company overhead was charged to the Circulation Company because its projected gross
revenues subsequent to the reorganization
were substantially less than in earlier years.

The Circulation Company and The Curtis
Publishing Company shared the services of a
common data processing department which
included not only machine services but also
the services of a substantial number of clerical

personnel who processed subscription
orders received (both the subscription
sales by the Circulation Company and
also subscription sales through direct
mail, agency, and other sources). The
data processing department also performed
all of the subscription fulfillment functions
for The Curtis Publishing Company. It is
extremely difficult to determine precisely
those costs for 1966 which relate to the
circulation sales effort on a basis compar-
able to 1967 because the charge tickets for
the data processing department for 1966
and prior years have been discarded. To
further complicate the matter the code of
accounts was revised in 1967. There is a
fairly significant difference between the
amounts charged to the Circulation Company
in 1966 under the prior method of accumu-
lating and allocating costs and what was
charged to the circulation sales effort in 1967.

In 1966 and 1967, certain bonuses
were paid to field representatives by Keystone
Readers' Service, Inc., which in prior years
had been reimbursed by The Curtis Publishing Company and normally are reimbursed by
Keystone's other client publishers. Management,
for certain reasons, decided that the substantial
bonuses paid to field representatives to promote
the sale of the Curtis magazines would no longer

be reimbursed to Keystone by Curtis, and, accordingly, the accounts for Keystone for the years 1966 and 1967 reflect a substantially lower commission from Curtis than might otherwise have been recorded had this decision not been made.

During a substantial portion of the period we are discussing, the combined circulation companies' receivables from The Curtis Publishing Company substantially exceeded the loans payable to the bank by the respective companies. However, the respective circulation companies were not reimbursed by Curtis for the substantial amounts of interest incurred in connection with these bank loans.

The Curtis Publishing Company and its domestic subsidiaries filed consolidated federal income tax returns. Because of the substantial losses and loss carry-overs of Curtis, no federal income taxes were paid during the period 1963 through 1967. The accounts of the respective circulation companies did not reflect a provision for taxes since the income from these operations was offset against the consolidated entity's losses and loss carry-overs.

It seems that I was always trying to muster forces to fight on two fronts simultaneously. While I was, on

the one hand, wrestling with the intricacies of accounting procedures (or their lack) I was, on the other hand,
trying to establish my concepts of "class" versus "mass."

One step towards the former was the acquisition
of a new publication. The purchase of *Status* magazine,
announced on July 16, was an effort to strengthen my
program and start putting my theory to work. Founded
by Igor Cassini in 1965 and two years later merged
with *Diplomat* magazine, *Status*'s circulation was then
145,000, a figure I hoped eventually to boost to
200,000. The magazine was still operating at a small
loss of about $40,000 a year, but since that figure
was well down from the $400,000 loss the first year
of publication, I felt the profit outlook was favorable.

The forty-two-year-old president of *Status*, Jules
J. Warshaw, was appointed publisher, and the new
editor was Frank Zachary, then art director of *Holiday*.
The plan was to develop a publication that was both
visually and textually exciting.

By mid-August it was apparent that we
would have to take other decisive steps to ease
Curtis' financial pressures. At the August first
Board of Directors meeting it was formally
noted that The First National Bank of Boston
was reluctant to extend payments further,
and that accordingly provision had to be made
for repayment of the portion of the company's debt to
the bank. A motion that Perfect take over the indebtedness and purchase the $12.5 million of Perfect Film

notes held by Curtis was approved. But the fact remained that Curtis still did not have sufficient available funds either to meet cash needs or debt payments.

The decision I then took, to sell *Ladies' Home Journal* and *American Home* was a calculated effort to acquire these funds, and the reasons that motivated this decision are complex.

*The Post* was not the only Curtis publication struggling for survival; the *Journal, American Home,* and *Holiday* also had their problems. In the case of the *Journal,* the flaws were hidden beneath a veneer of successes: the advertisers were supporting it; the editorial content was generally considered excellent; editor Jack Carter was considered one of the best in the business; and, in general, the *Journal* ranked at the top of the women's field. On the debit side, the magazine was far too costly to produce; the size was uneconomical; and the forty-two-pound high-quality paper was an unnecessary extravagance.

Moreover, the *Journal* was competing with *McCall's* for shrinking advertising dollars which were, moreover, being increasingly siphoned off by television. Where one magazine might have managed and even flourished, the two, under current economic conditions, were strangling each other.

*Ladies' Home Journal* and its companion magazine, *American Home,* represented a total of some ten million magazines to be produced each month. Ironically, the more magazines that were turned out, the greater

would be the loss. I felt that the only chance for the
two magazines' survival lay, not with Curtis, but with
some other publisher financially strong enough to
invest the necessary capital to redesign the formats
and to reduce costs.

My decision to sell the *Journal* and *American Home*,
especially the *Journal*, elicited shock and indignation
from most Curtis observers, and inevitably, reminders
of my initial promise *not* to do away with any of the
Curtis publications. It must be remembered that the
*Journal* was as much of an American institution as the
*Post*; indeed, it predated *The Post* and, having been
founded by Cyrus Curtis, had reached fruition under
his son-in-law, Bok. But after a long and careful evaluation of the situation, I reached the conclusion that
this step was the only way I could keep the magazines
alive.

Decisions were complicated by the Curtis accounting system's archaic methods of dealing with complex,
modern-day problems. It was impossible to determine
from the company's financial statements which magazines were making money and which ones were not.
Each magazine was made to bear a portion of company
overhead, and in all of the direct costing areas, overhead charges were added to them. All of the Curtis
publications carried all of the fixed costs through
allocations.

When I first came to Curtis, I wondered just *who*
was responsible for making these allocations. Whoever

he was, I decided that he must be the most important person in the company, holding as he did in his hands the profit and/or loss of each of the Curtis business segments.

However, this key role was assigned, not to one man, but to the accountants and engineers of Touche, Ross, Bailey & Smart's management service division.

What we had to do, and do quickly, was separate the various costs relating to the operation of the magazines and find those which were fixed.

We decided to break the magazine costs into two categories: those which could not be changed with volume or sales, or over which the company had very little day-to-day control, which we called *fixed* expenses, and those that varied with sales or volume which we called *variable* expenses.

The contributions to such company fixed costs for each magazine were shown separately. In this analysis, which was finished by the early part of July, 1968, it was evident that while the *Ladies' Home Journal* was making a small annual contribution of $1.5 million, *the fixed costs that could not be changed*—if we were going to continue to publish the *Journal* and *American Home*—were in the neighborhood of *$12 million*. Once the accounts were laid bare, the problem in non-accounting terms was, very simply, related to the negative overhead structure, which cost approximately $9 million a year to support. The overhead was centered mainly in the company's computer headquarters which were unquestionably needed to keep up with the 12 million-name subscriber lists of the *Ladies' Home Journal* and *American Home,* as well as with the operations essential in handling two such large magazines.

Obviously, this $12 million problem had to be dealt with first. If the structure were to be left to continue even through the balance of the year, all other plans would have to go by the board, since there was no way of finding a contribution from other magazines to help feed this fixed cost.

Since the *Journal* was the most efficiently operated of the Curtis publications, it was unlikely that its contribution could be improved. There was no alternative to getting rid of this fixed expense other than to dispose of the two magazines. The other magazines, *Holiday* and *The Post,* with one-million and three-million circulations respectively, were now small enough to handle on an outside service basis. Either we had to close both the *Ladies' Home Journal* and *American Home,* or we had to sell them. Otherwise, the fixed costs would drain the parent company of all its available funds, as they had already been doing relentlessly for years.

To find a buyer was another matter. The first publishers I approached were those who had previously indicated some interest in purchasing those magazines if they were ever put up for sale. First on my list was Time, Inc.; second, *McCall's;* third, *Times-Mirror.* Few prospective buyers, however, seemed to understand the

assumption of subscription liabilities. The *Journal* and
*American Home* owed their subscribers some $33 mil-
lion in magazines. In previous years, this money had
been collected by Curtis, but whether or not the subscriber received his magazine now would depend upon
new subscribers who, in future years, would be old
magazine subscribers, or—more importantly—upon the
advertising dollars received in order to subsidize the production of the magazines.

At the suggestion of a friend, I met with Charles
Bludhorn to discuss Gulf & Western's possible purchase
of the *Journal.* The G & W acquisition specialists with
whom I then negotiated were put off by the fact that,
in order to buy the magazine, they would have to
assume $33 million of subscription liabilities.

Evidently few people understood that this was
exactly what the publishing business was all about.
Moreover, the buyer would have to be prepared to
pump enormous amounts of money into the magazines in order to maintain the necessary flexibility to
compete with *McCall's* and keep the subscription list
at its rate base. During the past six or seven months,
when dollars were not available at Curtis, many of the
subscriptions had been allowed to lapse. Now there was
real need for a new infusion of money to bring the subscription rate base up to par.

The men at Time, Inc., were not interested; the
women's field was not their cup of tea. Moreover, they
felt with some justification that the problems that would

come with the magazines would be just too much to
handle.

Henry Bowes, then president of *McCall's,* was
more receptive. He enthusiastically supported my idea
of combining the two women's magazines, *McCall's*
and *Ladies' Home Journal*, into one new supermagazine.

Obviously, Bowes was undergoing problems similar to those we were facing with the *Journal*. We
agreed that, with the shrinking of the advertising
dollar, coupled with the menace of television
advertising, one magazine was sufficient to serve
the subscriber and the advertiser within any
special field. Encouraging as our meeting was,
however, for some reason the proposal to
join forces never got any further.

*Times-Mirror* gave the matter serious consideration, but even before an official decision had been
reached, it was obvious that this deal would never
come off.

It was while I was still involved in negotiations
with *McCall's* that Henry Silverman of Oppenheimer
& Co., told me that Edward R. Downe, Jr., head of
Downe Communications, Inc., was interested in buying *American Home*. A meeting was arranged in my
office with Downe and a financial adviser from the
firm of Carter, Berlind and Weill, Downe's investment
bankers. Thirty-eight-year-old Ed Downe was frank
and openminded. His company, which had recently

gone public, published the weekly newspaper supple-
ment, *Family Weekly*, and Ed was well versed in both
the mail order and publishing businesses. Downe Communications' stock was sold over-the-counter and had
gone from the opening price of $10 per share to
around $40 within a very brief period.

Ed Downe felt that the *Journal* and *American
Home*, once extricated from the straitjacket of Curtis's
traditional way of operating, could be published at
considerably less expense. He was optimistic, and as
a back-up to this optimism had prospects of raising
additional funds for operations, which he subsequently
did actually get his hands on.

He was also willing, as part of the deal, to let our
Sharon Hill plant continue printing the publications,
provided its prices were competitive; he agreed to sign
a printing contract at a substantial profit to Curtis
through June, 1969. Moreover, he agreed to leave the
single copy sales with the Curtis Circulation Company
for two years, plus some subscriptions with the Curtis
School Plan and Keystone. Most important of all, he
was willing to assume the subscription liabilities and
pay Curtis 100,000 shares of Downe Communications
stock in return for the copyrights to the magazines.
Since the company was to be given no receivables,
Downe realized he would have to pump literally millions of dollars into the magazines in order to bring
the subscriber list up to its rate base.

At the Curtis directors meeting called expressly to approve the sale, it was the general consensus of the Board that Curtis could not afford to speculate with the 100,000 shares (or about 9 percent of the company's common stock) of Downe Communications stock. Most of the directors felt that the stock was of dubious investment value and, therefore, arrangements should be made to sell it as soon as possible. Since this investment was letter stock and not freely marketable, it was necessary to find a purchaser who would be interested in buying these shares for a long-term investment. A sale was subsequently arranged with a group of mutual funds at $45 a share, cash. This money was then used to pay off the debt Curtis had incurred to Perfect.

As it turned out, the transaction was profitable all around and especially served to resuscitate *Ladies' Home Journal* and *American Home*, which otherwise would have rotted on the dying vine. Downe's page count for the first quarter moved ahead of *McCall's*. During the next year, Downe Communications stock went up as high as $180 a share.

As far as Curtis was concerned, even in retrospect, I cannot see how the company could otherwise have gotten through the summer and fall of 1968.

One major crisis had been met and Curtis was, for the moment at least, still in business.

# CHAPTER NINE

# COBWEBS OF THE PAST

*"This is all part of a plan to help Curtis sweep itself clean of the cobwebs of the past . . . ."*

Martin S. Ackerman, in an
interview with the press
October 15, 1968

# 9

There was a story going around when I first went with Curtis that one of the trustees had a curious method for coming to a decision. Whenever he could not make up his mind—which was apparently most of the time—he would turn to the minutes of meetings of several decades ago, which he had indexed for the purpose.

"Let's see," he would ask himself, "how did Curtis handle that problem back in 1937?"

Whether the story has any truth or not, it is at least indicative of the old-line Curtis corporate climate. "The way it has always been done" was a philosophy of life at the management level. No one ever wanted to initiate a *new* way of taking the lead, for fear of rocking the old boat.

Until I arrived at Curtis, power had been invested largely in the hands of directors who hailed from the Philadelphia Main Line establishment. Men like Moreau Brown, Walter Franklin, Bob Patterson, and Cary W. Bok were rooted like strong trees against the wind, fiercely loyal to The Curtis Publishing Company and its conservative traditions. The fact that none of them, except perhaps Bok, had any real financial reason for staying with the company was irrelevant. It was a question of *noblesse oblige,* of loyalty to an old friend facing hard times.

I do not have anything against tradition, loyalty and established friendships per se, but some of the best men can become too long tethered to antiquated ways of doing business. Some of these people were extremely dedicated. "Doc" Brown, for example, was especially so—an indefatigable worker who asked nothing in return. As a banker, he was well versed in modern business practices and methods, but nevertheless had to understand and work with the antiquated problems and complexities of the Curtis estate.

Then there was Bob Patterson and Walter Franklin.
Well intentioned though they were, they were finally
overwhelmed by the enormity of the financial crisis.
Patterson thought of himself as the representative of
the trustees and in almost every instance supported
their position. However, in matters of personal integrity, he was his own man.

Probably the man to whom the other directors
most deferred was Governor Driscoll. An old friend of
Cary Bok, he often conveyed messages from the latter,
in Maine, to the Board. Yet he always remained impar-
tial, fair, and dedicated to the company. I once asked
him why he had even accepted a Curtis directorship,
especially when there were so many headaches and so
little reward.

"I loved *The Saturday Evening Post* as a kid," he
replied. "I tried to help it with advertising when I was
at Warner-Lambert and I thought I might be helpful
in turning it around."

After I was elected president of Curtis, Driscoll
expressed the hope that *now* maybe we could get
down to the real business of trying to save *The Post*.
His confidence in us and what we were trying to do
was a major impetus behind our efforts to tackle this
gargantuan task.

Bob Hedbeurg was the paid representative of the
trustees on the Board of Directors. At first, hostile to

every management suggestion, he gradually became a
constructive member. He disagreed with me most of
the time, invariably adopting a non-negotiable position
in every controversy. His stand was that whereas he
was not in accord with our *methods*, he could not
help but approve of the *results*. In fact, he had no
other alternative.

Surrounded by men who had proven abilities,
strong integrity, and great loyalty to the company
itself, I at first asked myself the question, "How could
there be any basic problem here that has brought
Curtis to the brink of disaster?"

The answer was that *direction*—direction in the
sense of aiming at current and future objectives in a
realistic way—was lacking. Previous attempts at reorganization had failed dismally because of the hodge-
podge of elements and factors which ran counter to
each other. It was like trying to put together a team
of horses, with none of them heading in quite the
same direction. The old, traditional ways were in
conflict with new methods of administration, which
had to be applied just to do business with firms on
the outside. And every time a key executive wanted
to handle a project in a new way, there seemed to be
someone higher up who vetoed it.

But there were other, less obvious, weaknesses as
well.

For one thing, efforts to strengthen Curtis's economic structure had too often been motivated by the theory that reducing the staff and cutting overhead would automatically help the company make money. Invariably, such expediencies did little more than temporarily alleviate the situation.

There was no working plan for developing good managers and managerial talents within the company.

There were no sound controls over operating expenses.

The editorial and magazine staffers seemed to have no concept whatsoever of how to develop products that would be financially successful. They strove to improve their editorial packages, but only from the standpoint of style, content, and other purely editorial considerations.

Everyone at Curtis sat around waiting for miracles that never came. Management had grown complacent, assuming that since the company had been in business for generations it would continue forever.

Management had no guidelines on how to improve in key areas of responsibility.

Efficient and reliable accounting procedures for determining exactly how much money was being lost in any particular operation areas were nonexistent.

The fanfare associated with certain operations blinded management to fundamental weaknesses. The

company's Book Division, for instance, had been ac-
claimed a success and, as I said earlier, it did have enormous potential. But once we investigated it in depth,
we found that it was a real money loser. When my colleagues optimistically pointed to Time, Inc.'s Book
Division, supposedly so profitable that it was raking in
as much money as *Life* magazine once had, they over-
looked the fact that Time's Book Division had been a
going concern long before Curtis ever even contemplated following its example.

The same held true of the much-touted Enterprise and Audio-Visual Divisions, both of which were
steadily siphoning off money from the parent
company.

One of the biggest Curtis headaches, and one
which had been virtually ignored, was the computer
center located in Philadelphia. The center had been
badly handled from its inception, and was costing
Curtis some $8 million per year. Curtis had made the
initial mistake of buying rather than leasing its equipment—and the wrong equipment at that. Curtis had
reportedly bought the equipment from a company
which used more advertising space in Curtis magazines
than did competitive bidders. Fixed expenses inciden-
tal to the operation of the center were huge, and a
constant obstacle. Caught in a web of past errors and
mismanagement, the real miracle was that The Curtis
Publishing Company had managed to survive this long!

On September 29, I reported at a Board of Directors meeting that the sale of the *Ladies' Home Journal* and *American Home* had been completed, and that 100,000 shares of Downe stock, transferred to Perfect Film & Chemical on the loan account, had been sold by Perfect to a group of investors for $4.5 million.

Perfect had advanced another $2,850,000 to Curtis under the Basic Bank Agreement and was to exercise its rights under the agreement to take title to certain collateral of the company in order that Curtis might meet its September loan payments. This seemed the only realistic step that could be taken at the time to avoid the virtual cessation of Curtis activities.

At the October fourteenth meeting of the Executive Committee of the Board of Directors, I announced that Perfect Film intended to transfer *Holiday*, *Status*, and *The Saturday Evening Post* to a new company, to be named "The Saturday Evening Post Company," in exchange for 100,000 shares of common stock of that company. This was part of a plan, I said, "to help Curtis sweep itself clean of the cobwebs of the past"— a figure of speech which, to judge from the frequency with which it was quoted by the press, seemed to appeal to the nation's journalists.

The new company, in which Curtis was to have a $5 million investment, was to be further refinanced with at least $10 million in new capital from outside sources. The plan was to provide enough capital so that the new company could not only expand and develop the three existing magazines, but ultimately acquire other publishing and communications properties as well.

With the reorganization and formation of the new company, along with a more practical approach to printing and paper-making contracts and arrangements, I was optimistic. I confidently informed the press that I was certain the future of *The Post* was assured; that it would become a profitable magazine; and that the advertising contracts would exceed our expectations. We had freed Curtis from the straitjacket of "its own bureaucracy," and now there would be a reasonable degree of flexibility, as well as a means of detouring the old problem of costs which were too frozen and which did not have enough variables.

In the course of my tenure at Curtis, I had evolved a philosophy of publishing which was the subject of an address I delivered about this time at the 51st Annual Conference of the Direct Mail Advertising Association. The text was subsequently reproduced in part in *Direct Marketing*, a magazine devoted to business communications.

Magazine and magazine publishers have, for a long time, been very profitable and very successful. However, like all industries, publishing is changing. Publishers, the once

great Curtis Publishing Company, the
Time, Inc's., and the others, are becoming
aware that the things we did years ago are
not the things that will sustain us in the
future.

Publishers suffered a great shock with
the advent of television and reacted by trying to outnumber television. I think today
we see that decision was wrong. The original concept of publishing was based on two
sources of income—income from subscriptions and income from advertising. The
balanced approach of an income publishing
statement was extremely important.

The numbers game, the subscription
revenue game, the audience theory, and all
the rest are coming to an end. Why? Because there probably are not in the United
States as many people who want to read magazines as publishers thought there were. There
are only so many readers. There are only so
many people who are interested in magazines.

Television is different. Television is entertainment. Television is free. Television is a
commodity which is altogether different from
magazines. What is happening in the publishing business and what you will see happening
in the future is an understanding of the
changing nature of the commodity. We must

reevaluate where we are going and decide
how to be profitable. There's always been a
great sway in the publishing business between
the advertising side and the editorial side
called "editorial integrity." But the editors
are becoming quite aware that unless they
are profitable, successful magazines that do
do a job, there will be no magazines.

It was both my conviction and hope that, with
240 years of service and dedication behind it, *The
Saturday Evening Post* could be restored to its historic
position of preeminence. But in order to accomplish
this, the magazine and Curtis Publishing Company
would have to move with the times. The real test of
any magazine, after all, is whether or not people are
reading it, and one way of determing this is by using
magazines as carriers for ads for direct mail response.
"The Carriers Theory of Publishing," as I saw it, was
the trend of the future.

If you take *Playboy* and look through
it, what do you find? Carrier direct mail advertising for its own products. If you take
*Esquire,* or any magazine of any substance
from *Life* to *Time* to *Newsweek,* you find
many things being done within the framework of the "carrier" theory. The most important thing for us to realize, is that we
must sit down and examine where we are

going. What can we do? How do we get
there and how can we keep the media going?
One of the interesting things I have discovered, since I have been in publishing and also
in mail order, is an understanding of the
sources of income.

All magazines are struggling for survival, and
many which might otherwise not have made it are alive
today thanks to direct mail advertising. It is my opinion that had Curtis applied this theory early enough
in the game, *The Post* would still be with us.

But that was just the trouble; at Curtis, it was
always too late in the game. A critique appearing in
the January, 1969, *Magazine Industry Newsletter* re-
capitulated the problems with which we were grap-
pling:

The Curtis complex supplied everything
from the tree for the paper mills to the newsstands
which sold the publications, excluding ink manufacturing. There was no desire to diversify:
Curtis turned down an entire TV network in
1947, ABC, for $3.5 million; excluded itself
from book publishing through its arrangement
to distribute Bantam books and own some
stock in the venture; failed to enter the spe-
cialty magazine field, either consumer or
trade, when there were indications that this

could be a profit center. The changing social climate was treated as an inconvenience—like missing the regular commuter train. There would be another train shortly, they assumed, so there was little purpose in fretting; besides, revenues were continually rising. The quintessence of Curtis' policy was expressed in the purchase of the New York & Pennsylvania Paper Company. The paper mill provided Curtis with paper that was inferior to what competitive publications were able to buy at a lower cost. The acquisition was snuggled in labrynthian clauses which committed Curtis to the purchase of unused capacities. By this time, too, Curtis' management had created enough departments and fuzzy lines of responsibility to qualify as a government agency.

Just when we thought we were seeing our way clear, we found ourselves trapped in a tangle of cobwebs that had accumulated through too many years of neglect.

# CHAPTER TEN

# POST MORTEM

*"Post's Mortem: Death by Failure to Specialize. There was a wake for The Saturday Evening Post Thursday. . .the mourners were journalists."*

*Los Angeles Times*
Jan. 17, 1969

# 10

By January, 1969, it was evident to everyone that *The Saturday Evening Post*, born in 1821 and "once the multicolored gospel of American-style living on six million coffee tables," was, in fact, going to fold. It was officially announced that the February 8 issue would be the last.

Letters poured into Curtis from readers all over the world, offering suggestions which ranged from the bizarre to the brilliant on how we might salvage the

magazine. Long after *The Post* was dead and gone even,
one reader put forth a plan for bringing it, like Lazarus,
back from the grave:

> You are having problems with readers
> who say they do not want *Life*—or any
> other magazine—as a substitute for *The Post;*
> yet you say you can no longer continue to
> publish it. There is a simple alternative.
> Start publishing facsimile copies of maga-
> zine issues that have appeared down through
> the generations, going right back 147 years
> if necessary. I'd love to see what appeared,
> say, at the turn of the century, or back in
> the days of the Gay Nineties.

It was not such a wild idea at that.

The *Los Angeles Times* reported that at the
"funeral" it was I who administered the last rites, and
"the mourners were journalists." They recalled my
statement the preceding April to the effect that "as
long as I am here there'll not be a last issue of *"The
Saturday Evening Post."* Never were words so bitterly
or regretfully eaten.

With the possible exception of *Look* and *Life*,
television had taken over the mass audience magazine
dollar, and in order to survive, magazines had to
address themselves to a specialized audience. In my
opinion, one of the big mistakes magazine publishers

made was to attempt to beat out their electronic com-
petitor by sheer force of numbers, since it was obvious
that people would rather watch than read. TV is for
the masses; magazines for the special groups. Our efforts
to capture this special market had nevertheless failed—
perhaps because they came too late.

The press responded to *The Post*'s death with nostalgia and emotion. The American scene may have
changed at a breathtaking pace, but there still existed
an enormous number of people who recalled a happier,
simpler day, and to them *The Post* was more than a
magazine—it was a symbol of their own vanished youth,
of the peculiar mixture of "corn" and sophistication
that had marked another, earlier era.

"It is a disturbing and saddening time to those who
make their livelihood from the printed word when a
newspaper or magazine dies," commented the *Spring-
field Daily News.* "The demise of *The Saturday Evening
Post*, however, is more than just the end of a venerable and respected publication. It is the death knell of
the way of American life for which *The Post* was a
sentimental and articulate spokesman."

Another newspaper mourned, "Gone are the covers
of red-blooded Americans by Norman Rockwell. No
more will 'Post Scripts' bring a chuckle. Tugboat
Annie's in drydock for good and Alexander Botts has
sold his last Earthworm Tractor."

A small-town newspaper in Pennsylvania dramatically depicted the final issue of the magazine draped
in black and lying in a silk-lined coffin. The epitaph
read, "The people subscribed. . .but the advertisers
didn't advertise."

To judge from the magazines and newspapers,
American journalists, without exception, had served
their apprenticeships as salesboys for *The Post*. They
recalled that prior to World War I, they paid two and
a half cents a copy and sold it for five cents. By World
War II, however, *The Saturday Evening Post* boys were
a vanishing breed. These younger journalists tended to
recall *The Post* instead as a kind of literary mentor.

Columnist Stewart Alsop wrote, "The last great
mass market for fiction has closed down. A lot of good
nonfiction writing is still being written of course, but
in this writer's passionately prejudiced opinion, good
writing is menaced by television, which threatens to
engulf the written word like a blob from outer space
in one of television's own idiot pleasures. The decay
of the written word of which *The Post*'s death is a
symbol is surely a tragedy and maybe not a very
small tragedy."

*The Post* had, after all, served as a vehicle for
some of the greats in American letters—Harriet Beecher
Stowe, Jack London, Edgar Allen Poe, James Fenimore
Cooper, Bret Harte, Stephen Crane, Theodore Dreiser,
O. Henry, Thomas Wolfe, Joseph Conrad, Edna Ferber,
John Hersey, and John O'Hara. The list of *Post* writers

reads like a college course in twentieth century American literature and, more important, they had brought first-rate literature to the masses.

Among the mourners, however, there were those whose eulogies were tinged with bitterness. Norman Rockwell, the artist most closely associated, traditionally, with the magazine breathed a sigh of relief. "Hell," he said, in an interview, "I was glad that it died. The magazine was sick for so long, it was a relief when it finally went—like the relief you feel when an old friend who has suffered so much in an illness finally goes."

The Washington, D.C. *Evening Star* described *The Post*'s old age as "not a particularly graceful one. Like a dowager touched with senility, the old girl shortened her skirts, put on a little too much paint, and tried to learn the new dances. It didn't work."

The *Star* added, "it was never a truly fashionable magazine. The smart thing was always to look down on *The Post* as middle-class and square. While the highbrows sneered, millions of readers bought *The Post* and got their money's worth."

The Cincinnati *Inquirer* was less reverent. "There was a time decades back when the failure of *The Saturday Evening Post* would have been a real national misfortune with sorrowful repercussions in most walks of life." The magazine's "suicide" it attributed to the cutback in circulation and the fact that it was "uprooted from Philadelphia and turned into a foreigner in Manhattan."

The *Inquirer* asserted that the days had long since passed when *The Post* was a top market for good fiction. Granting that its articles were solid and constructive, they had deteriorated, said the paper, to the point where the magazine was complimenting the Mafia on its ability to "get things done," and its once beautifully executed covers had degenerated into kindergarten paste-ups.

The critic from Cincinnati zeroed in on the January 25 issue, "a sorry epitaph for a once great magazine." The cover in question was a composite of the covers of pornographic magazines, in tandem with a lead article on "How Barney Rossett publishes dirty books for fun and profit." Citing a "pointless" article by Arthur Miller on a chance encounter with Lucky Luciano in Rome and one entitled "The Enigma of President Nixon," which it dispensed with as "Nixon baiting," The *Inquirer* concluded: "It is a sour note upon which a once mighty trumpet is stilled."

*Post* editors emerged out of oblivion to add their voice to the dirge. Ben Hibbs who had retired as editor in 1961 attributed his editorial success to a "sort of God-given instinct for what people like to read. That's an egotistic thing to say but I did have it—perhaps because I was one of the people. I was a poor kid, had to work my way through college and so on. I had a feeling, I think, for what interested the great middle-class Americans and I had a very deep feeling about America itself. My

wife also said I had an American Flag tatooed on my
chest."

Hibbs' concept of *The Post* was a family magazine which any twelve-year-old kid could pick up with
his mother's approval.

"We published some very startlingly plain articles
on important subjects," Hibbs reminisced, "but we did
it in a decent way."

During his editorship, the magazine had also been
successful from an advertising point of view, until some
of the big agencies decided that *The Post* was no
longer what in advertising jargon is called "the hot
book." The ad agencies, he said, are sheep—"a few of
them start doing something and they all start running
in the same direction."

Then television entered the picture and "so
things got a little skimpy in the advertising field and
they got more skimpy in my last year, and since then
you know what's happened."

The advertising publications also got into the
act. *Advertising Age* commented, "Much of the general press material has been heavily nostalgic, as well
it might when one considers the prominent role
that *The Post* played in the leisure life of Americans from the turn of the century up through
the 1940s."

*Ad Age* proffered its own *Post* autopsy. Back
in the '20s, when The Curtis Publishing Company was
in its heyday, the company treasurer, Walter Fuller,
discovered that Curtis could save a million dollars by

using Cuneo printing instead of its own printing facilities. Cyrus Curtis, on being shown the enormous
savings which could be effected by such a move, scoffed:
"We are not interested in saving a million dollars."

The editorial also cited the fact that the Curtis
magazines in the Roaring Twenties accounted for two
dollars of every five dollars spent in the U.S. for
national advertising, and commented that this early
success was "the beginning of its undoing, because
it blinded the publication both editorally and on the business side to any need to change as the times changed. Instead of keeping abreast or a step or two ahead of the contemporary scene, *The Post* simply continued doing business in the same old manner and eventually the times
left the magazine wallowing in their wake."

Recent efforts to improve the magazine, according
to this editorial, actually did result in a superior editorial
product—but unfortunately it was too late in the day.

The impact of *The Post*'s demise on the magazine world was not without its observers. "Was the
death of *The Saturday Evening Post* magazine a signal
of magazine industry trouble or an exception?
asked the Chicago *Tribune*. Paul Harper, chairman
of Needham, Harper & Steers, Inc. ad agency, considered *The Post* tragedy an exception in an era of
growth that he predicted would be "the brightest in

its history." Other writers, however, did not share Harper's optimism, pointing out a long trend which began with the death of *The American* magazine in late 1956 and continued through the end of *Collier's* in 1957, the original *Coronet* in 1961, *Reporter* in late 1968, not to mention other defunct magazines such as *Literary Digest, American Mercury, Liberty,* and a host of lesser ones.

Vice-President Spiro T. Agnew was one of the few commentators among the mourners who drew a laugh. Admitting that vice-presidents suffer from an acute lack of identity he said, "I've run into hard luck occasionally. *The Saturday Evening Post* planned a cover story on me for the April issue."

There was no trace of the emotion and nostalgia that gripped the American public at news of *The Post*'s demise in the minutes of the Special Joint Meeting of the Board of Directors of The Curtis Publishing Company, held January 6, 1969. To the contrary, the drama behind the drama was couched in extremely cut and dried business-like language:

> The Executive Committee. . .had met. . .and had voted to recommend to the Board of Directors of The Saturday Evening Post Company (Sepco) that the publication of *The Saturday Evening Post* be discontinued.

A discussion then ensued with respect to
this matter, and during the course of such
discussion, it was pointed out that the
unfulfilled subscription liabilities of *The
Saturday Evening Post* totaled approximately
$18 million; that the necessary increase in
advertising lineage in the magazine did not
materialize; that on the basis of present
budgetary figures an operating loss of
approximately $3 million was indicated for
the current fiscal year if publication is
continued; and that the financial condition
of both companies was such that they
could not continue to sustain such losses.
It was noted that if the equity of shareholders is to be preserved, this drain must
be eliminated and the assets of the companies employed in areas where a profit
potential exists. It was further noted that,
in the course of the last eight years, Curtis
had expended approximately $35 million
of new money in an effort to save what
everyone regards as an established American
institution but to no avail.

A question was raised by Mr. Hedberg
as to whether it might be desirable to
postpone a decision for a couple of weeks
to ascertain whether the magazine could be
sold to a third party. Messrs. Mills and
Driscoll stated that there was no reason to
delay the action since opportunities to purchase the magazine had been open to others

for the last two years and no offers
had been received. It was also pointed out
that the opportunity to make arrangements
with other magazines to take over unfulfilled subscription liabilities might evaporate
unless action were taken promptly. In
response to a question as to whether dis-
continuance of the magazine required
approval of the shareholders of Curtis,
Mr. Gould observed that the Board not
only had the right but the duty to take
action to conserve the assets of Curtis.
Unless such a step were taken, the equity
of the shareholders would be dissipated
through operating losses and unfulfilled
subscription liabilities.

Following these proceedings, I then presented
to the Board a proposal from Grove Press, Inc., to continue publication of *The Post,* as well as another
proposal for purchase of $3½ million worth of stock
from LIN Broadcasting Corporation which, "given
good management and adequate financing," would
afford the Saturday Evening Post Company an opportunity to enter the broadcasting business with favorable chances of success.

While the LIN offer was worth serious consideration, Barney Rosset, president of Grove Press, had
offered neither cash nor Grove stock, and was further-
more unwilling to assume any obligations whatsoever.
Referring to our decision to discontinue publication

as "murder," he claimed to base his offer on the
grounds that my colleagues and I had "no moral right
to allow an American institution to die when such is
not necessary." To me, his offer of assistance smacked
outrageously of a gross publicity stunt.

It has been said that my fundamental problem
with Cary Bok and the Curtis trustees began with the
end of *The Saturday Evening Post*. Robert Hedberg
and Robert Patterson, both representatives of the
Curtis trustees on the Board of Directors, constituted
my only link with them. At the meeting to vote on
the closing of the publication, Hedberg informed the
directors that he had been instructed to vote against
the motion, but that, since as an individual he was
in favor of the motion, he was going to abstain.

We who were behind the scenes wanted to see
*The Post* die even less than the public and journalists who mourned its end so eloquently. Why, then,
did we have to reach this decision? When the Saturday Evening Post Company was organized, I made it
clear to both the institutional investors who had put
up $10 million and the Curtis Board that unless the
magazine could have at least 1,000 pages of paid
advertising for the year ended December 31, 1969,
there would be no other alternative to closing down
the magazine. We had provided during the latter
part of 1968 for an extremely careful analysis of
the way in which advertising pages were to be booked
for the year 1969. Since advertising budgets were
allocated during the latter part of 1968 for the first

six months of 1969, by Christmas of 1968 we should
have been in a position to tell pretty much how the
first six months of the year would look.

I assured Steve Kelly, the publisher, Bill Emerson,
the editor, and all members of the Curtis Board that I
personally would watch the progress of the advertising
pages, and that, moreover, I had set up a monitoring
system with the help of Touche, Ross, Bailey & Smart's
management service division, which would project the
pages based upon careful budgeting and planning. By
the end of 1968, we had cut all the expenses we could
from *The Post* and still managed to publish a decent
magazine. Having experimented with better-priced
subscriptions, we thought income could be brought
in from this source. I did not see how the company
could survive a loss of more than $1 million from *The
Post* for 1969.

Projections from the Advertising Department
under both Culligan and Clifford had been invariably
favorable, but somehow something always happened
in between the estimate and the actuality, and the
loss for the year turned out to be greater than anticipated. Although it was my feeling that *The Post*
deserved a chance, I could not risk the whole of The
Saturday Evening Post Company or, for that matter,
The Curtis Publishing Company, on our ability to sell
the pages.

My *modus operandi* has always been that, having
set goals, you must map out an alternative plan to
follow in the event of failure. As president of The

Curtis Publishing Company as well as of The Saturday
Evening Post Company, I did not feel duty-bound to
retain *The Post* at all cost. Provided we didn't lose
too much of the capital of The Saturday Evening Post
Company and that we could adjust the manufacturing
and paper facilities quickly enough, I felt there was a
chance for all arms of the company to revise themselves and move forward under the master plan.

The projections we had made also showed quite
clearly that the magazine had to be watched with
extreme care. The expenses each month were so inflex-
ible that little could be done to reduce them. Success
or failure depended upon the income account, and our
only source was advertising since revenue from subscriptions and newsstand sales was comparatively
insignificant.

Touche, Ross, Bailey & Smart prepared a graph
indicating the effect of each ten pages of advertising
on the budget forecasts. The graph showed that at
900 pages we would lose, as I estimated, $1 million
off budget, and for each 50 pages thereafter, it
would mean an additional million dollar loss. With
only 750 pages of advertising, we could expect to
lose anywhere between three and four million dollars.
Then, if we had to fold *The Post* at the end of the
year, the closing costs would be approximately
another million dollars.

Many of the pages in Steve Kelly's estimate
may have been morally committed for, but there
were no bona-fide orders on hand; thus we had to

expect substantial shrinkage from the so-called "committed orders." Based upon past experience, I presumed
that the Sales Department would be optimistic in its
order count, whereas Touche, Ross, Bailey & Smart
would be pessimistic. I estimated that if we could get
750 pages we would have no alternative but to close
the magazine; on the other hand, if we could get 900
pages, we could keep it going.

By late December it was evident to me that since
we could not reach the desired goals, an emergency
session for the presentation of the facts before the
Boards of Directors of Curtis and The Saturday Evening
Post Company would have to be called. This was to be
the first time in the long history of Curtis that an
honest appraisal of *The Post* in terms of the entire
company was to be made, no matter how undesirable
the consequences. Having made every conceivable
attempt to salvage the magazine, it was now clear
that further efforts would only jeopardize the company as a whole. The prognosis for The Curtis Publishing Company and The Saturday Evening Post
Company was hopeful, provided that its critically
ill limb, *The Saturday Evening Post*, was removed
before the infection spread to the still healthy body.

Mr. James MacIntosh, senior member of the
firm of Morgan, Lewis and Bocklis, the attorneys
to later represent Cary Bok in his inane lawsuit
against the other directors and me, spoke at this
meeting of the Executive Committee. MacIntosh
held that the Board of Directors of both The Curtis

Publishing Company and The Saturday Evening Post
Company had no legal authority to close down *The
Saturday Evening Post*; that rather, the decision was
up to the Curtis trustees and the rest of the shareholders. In a telephone conversation with MacIntosh,
Milton Gould countered that, to the contrary, the
directors not only had the right but the duty to close
down *The Post* if the facts so warranted. Moreover,
it was incumbent upon the directors to preserve
what assets they could once the facts indicated that
continuation of the publication would result in severe
losses. Needless to say, the trustees were in full agreement with MacIntosh, but it was my considered opinion that, having made a careful presentation of the
facts, and having done everything within my power
to salvage the magazine, it was now up to the Curtis
Board of Directors to make the final decision.

The rest is, of course, history.

# CHAPTER ELEVEN

# THE AFTERMATH

*"Because it wasn't the magazine
that stopped fitting into today's
scheme of living; even in its
worst days millions of people
bought it and read it and bitched
about it when their copies failed
to arrive. What didn't fit was The
Curtis Publishing Company's
business philosophy."*

Editorial on *The Saturday Evening Post*
*Esquire*, October, 1969

# 11

Ackerman's ideas for the salvation of *The Post* were good ones, but they were at least three years too late. Within three months he ordered *The Post* out of its costly circulation struggle, arranged to dump his unwanted names on *Life*, and tried to inspire another 'new era' of sophistication in the editorial content. But Curtis implacably botched the job Ackerman wanted to perform. . . .

"The magazine, meanwhile, improved dramatically in its last year, although its graphic originality and make-up remained spotty. . . . But Curtis had abused it and its readers too long, and even under Ackerman, with his reasonable prescription for its revival, the smothering hug of the inefficient company was too strong to break."

The words are those of Don A. Schanche, an able editor who joined *The Post* in 1960 and lived through some of the frustrations. I quote them, not to give myself a pat on the back, but as one more item of evidence that the Curtis economic climate, like that of the moon, was just too hostile for executive survival. On March 4, 1969, I officially resigned as president and director of The Curtis Publishing Company.

After closing down *The Post* I served a stint as publisher of *Holiday*, but I never was and never intended to be an editor.

Sixty-year-old G.B. McCombs, who had joined Curtis before I was even born, succeeded me as temporary chief executive. McCombs' tenure lasted for exactly five weeks. He resigned in mid-April when the presidency was taken over by Philip P. Kalodner, a thirty-eight-year-old Philadelphia lawyer who thereby realized a long-time ambition. Kalodner, according to *The Wall Street Journal*, "was said to have beseeched fellow directors at a stormy seven-hour board meeting . . . to elect him president to succeed Mr. McCombs. The other directors declined to do so, but could offer no candidates of their own willing to step in and take over."

Kalodner's reign exceeded his predecessor's by two weeks. Seven weeks after he assumed the presidency, he was deposed by Arthur Murphy, Jr.

formerly of Time, Inc., and *McCall's.* Now it was
Kalodner's turn to bring charges against Curtis, especially the trustees who, one newspaper reported, he
accused of being "out to liquidate the firm."

While the turmoil continued to rage on at Curtis,
I turned my thoughts and energies to Perfect Film &
Chemical Corporation.

I have always been interested in failure-to-success
stories, and even now, I cannot write off the Curtis
adventure as a total misadventure. After all, Curtis had
not lost out altogether. As I told *Business Week,*
"Curtis has a tremendous amount of good assets which,
if marshaled in the right direction, could accomplish
a great deal." Perfect had not lost any money in its
efforts to salvage *The Post,* and as for me—well, even
though, as I told a national journalism society, I was
a "Johnny-come-lately to publishing" and had "made
some mistakes." I had learned an enormous amount.

*Business Week* commented, "While he has flunked
his literary survival test, Ackerman apparently has passed
with flying colors the financial test of manipulating the
Curtis assets." The February issue of *New York* magazine took the opposite tack: "Ackerman," the article
headlined, "viewed himself as a teacher and *The Saturday Evening Post* had flunked." The same article
then called me a "press lord":

> Marty did like being a press lord. He
> admits that the "fun" of publishing *The Post*
> led him to involve himself more deeply and
> spend more money in trying to save it than

he would have otherwise. "If *The Post*
had been a drugstore, I would have
locked it up in April," he says. "Statis-
tically, I could have made a lot more
money doing other things." His friends
knew the press lord feeling would be
brief. "Marty likes the glamor and
excitement of going quickly from deal
to deal," says one.

Author Chris Welles went on to observe that
whereas "most builders of corporate empires have
multiskilled management teams in the home office
who can be dispatched on repair jobs," I was, in
effect, a "one-man show." Certainly at Curtis, this
was not the case, since we sought advice from a
multitude of "experts" in all manner of fields. But
the *New York* article ended with at least this kudo
from Milton S. Gould: ". . . Curtis is not bank-
rupt. It's $10 million richer. The creditors are happy.
I'm happy. We're all happy. Marty's a great kid. He
did a good job. He's one of the ablest, most dynamic
human beings I know. What else do you want to
know?"

There were other kudos, too. My associates, said
an article in *The Wall Street Journal*, "are quick to
point out that while Marty may be down, he's far from
out. 'The thing about Marty is that he always lands on
his feet and keeps swinging,' says William G. Prime,

vice-president of Equity Research Associates and
neither Ackerman friend nor foe."

Yet despite it all, the parting was quite bitter—at
least on the Curtis side of the fence. Every one, it
seemed, was taking any measure, no matter how desperate, to try to prove that some one other than
himself was at fault. By mid-January of 1969, the
threat of lawsuits hovered over Curtis like a swarm
of locusts. With the demise of *The Post*, employees
facing the spectre of unemployment grumbled that
severance compensations were inadequate. Subscribers
who were dissatisfied with the new subscription
arrangements went through the courts to demand
cash refunds. But these suits were anticipated and,
compared with the explosions that were in the off-
ing, were merely the detonations of toy cap pistols.

Early in the week of February 3, the trustees of
the Cyrus H. K. Curtis Estate had asked for my resigna-
tion as president and director of The Curtis Publishing
Company, as well as the resignations of Milton S. Gould,
director; E. Eugene Mason, secretary and director; and
G. B. McCombs, executive vice president and director.
Two other directors, Harry C. Mills and Alfred E.
Driscoll, had already tendered their resignations in a ges-
ture of disapproval of the way things were going at Curtis.

The trustees' letter to the Curtis board, accusing
me of "conflict of interest," was delivered, whether
by plan or coincidence, while I was vacationing in

Puerto Rico. This action was followed by several lawsuits, against me as well as against three of the directors
and Curtis Publishing Company itself. None of the
charges had any basis in truth. Yet the situation reached
such a sorry state that an examination of the proceedings had to be made by a special committee and a
report issued.

The result was the now famous "Pinkham Report,"
prepared by the New York law firm of Colton and
Pinkham, under the direction of Spencer Pinkham, a
specialist in corporate transactions, and published in
its entirety in the Appendix of this book. In brief,
the conclusions it reached were that there was no
basis for lawsuit, no evidence of "fraud" or "overreaching" and that legal action would be detrimental
to all concerned. Indeed, the report ended with the
following words:

> . . . prosecution of these cases, in the
> blaze of publicity which cannot be avoided,
> is now doing and will continue to do vastly
> more harm to Curtis, Perfect and Sepco (The
> Saturday Evening Post Company) than can
> ever be recovered for Curtis at the end of
> the road.

Although the lawsuits were all either thrown out
of court or withdrawn, I mention these actions here
simply as further evidence of the lack of a realistic

management philosophy and the tendency to flail
meaninglessly about whenever the company was swept
into a new crisis.

The Curtis Publishing Company, as Milton Gould
once observed, was "the greatest corporate disaster in
the history of America." Many men before me had
tried with varying degrees of success to put the company back on its feet, but none had really succeeded;
to the contrary, Curtis had a way of destroying those
who tried the hardest to help it. In retrospect, the
irony of the Curtis-Ackerman affair is that it still
represents to me one of my major achievements in
the corporate world, in spite of the frustrations,
failures and disappointments that marked those ten
short months when I was at the Curtis helm.

I marshalled to the task some of the best executive talent available; not only the management team
at Perfect and the management services division of
Touche, Ross, Bailey & Smart which had helped me
salvage Perfect in the early '60s, but I also sought
the opinions of those who had climbed to the top
of the publishing field, men from Time, Inc., Hearst,
and Cowles.

The rough-and-tumble of publishing is glossed
over with a veneer of glamor and prestige; but the
fact of the matter is that few areas of activity are
so completely at the mercy of the conflicting forces
of our dynamically changing society.

The repercussions of the Curtis affair do not end here. It is impossible to say how, or in what way, they may affect the future of Curtis. For my part, I cannot prophecy how they will affect my own future. In the corporate field, as elsewhere, the safer you play the game, the fewer risks you take. Perhaps, as many had advised, Curtis and *The Saturday Evening Post* should have been left to die their own deaths, in their own way. Going back to the remarks made by Milton G. Gould when I first expressed interest in Curtis, it is clear that my attempt to salvage the company was "like boarding the *Titanic*." It was too late in the day. The great mammoth was already inflexibly on course; and the iceberg lay waiting.

Perhaps the challenge was too great for any one to face.

*I did not think so then. And, oddly enough, I do not think so now.*

# APPENDIX

# THE PINKHAM REPORT

Complete text of the report
referred to in Chapter Eleven,
*"The Aftermath"*

COLTON & PINKHAM

212 RE 2-2672

ATTORNEYS                    CABLE "COLTONLAW"

120 BROADWAY

NEW YORK, N.Y. 10005

March 25, 1969

Philip P. Kalodner, Esq.,
    Messrs. Thomas S. Hyland and
    Lawrence Kessel

Gentlemen:

On March 10, 1969 you were constituted by the
Board of Directors of The Curtis Publishing Company
(Curtis) as a Committee to examine and report to
such Board

"as to the validity of all of the allegations of
the complaint filed by Cary W. Bok against
Martin S. Ackerman, Perfect Film & Chemical
Corporation, E. Eugene Mason, Milton S.
Gould, Downe Communications, Inc., The
Saturday Evening Post Company, G. B. McCombs
and The Curtis Publishing Company for the
purpose of determination by the Board what

action should be taken with respect to
said Complaint."

The undersigned was simultaneously appointed counsel
for such Committee.

Since such appointment, I have endeavored to
familiarize myself to some extent with the proceedings which have been had in such law suit and the
facts which underlie the allegations contained in the
complaint.

This letter is designed to report to you the results
of my endeavors. If it contains any suggestions as to
actions by the Committee, the same are intended to
be no more than tentative thoughts, subject to your
consideration and action and, thereafter, to action by
the Board.

1. <u>The Years Prior to 1968</u>.

Before discussing the complaint itself, some
history and background would seem to be indicated.

Curtis has for some years been operated by a
Board of Directors and a Management, largely selected
by descendants of Cyrus H. K. Curtis, the founder of
Curtis, and Trustees under his Will, including the plain-
tiff. Its recent operational history has not been happy.

Its earnings and net worth for the last few years have
been as follows:

|      | Net Earnings (Loss) | Net Worth     |
|------|---------------------|---------------|
| 1956 | $  6,230,000        | $36,551,000   |
| 1957 |    6,240,000        |  38,799,000   |
| 1958 |    2,510,000        |  44,174,000   |
| 1959 |    3,960,000        |  47,694,000   |
| 1960 |    1,630,000        |  46,341,000   |
| 1961 |   (4,190,000)       |  46,849,000   |
| 1962 |  (18,977,000)       |  27,932,000   |
| 1963 |   (3,379,000)       |  24,539,000   |
| 1964 |  (13,936,000)       |   9,656,000   |
| 1965 |   (2,613,000)       |  20,642,000   |
| 1966 |      394,000        |  21,526,000   |
| 1967 |   (4,839,000)       |  16,854,000   |

The loss in 1965 is before a non-recurring gain of $14,306,000 arising from the sale in that year of property in Canada for approximately $24,000,000. The net worth in 1965, 1966, and 1967 necessarily includes such windfall gain. Accordingly, but for the sale of such real property, the net worth of Curtis in the last three years, included in the above tabulation, would have been:

|      | Net Worth   |
|------|-------------|
| 1965 | $6,336,000  |
| 1966 | 7,220,000   |
| 1967 | 2,548,000   |

It will thus be seen that between 1960 and 1967 Curtis lost a total of about $44,000,000, excluding the $14,000,000 gain on the sale of real property, and over $30,000,000, giving full credit for such nonrecurring gain.

It should also be borne in mind that, although the balance sheet of Curtis as at December 31, 1967, shows an aggregate net worth or equity for the stockholders of $16,854,000, nevertheless, the Preferred Stock is cumulative and its liquidating value as at December 31, 1967 was $34,321,000. Accordingly, it is clear that for a substantial period of time there has been no equity in the Common Stock and the Preferred Stock has been substantially under water.

Without setting forth details, the accounting data
which has been furnished to me indicates that the
primary magazines published by Curtis or its subsidiaries, such as the Saturday Evening Post, Ladies Home
Journal and Holiday, have been losing money. It is
quite clear that Curtis' cash position was inadequate
($425,000 as at December 31, 1967) and that it had
surely used up its borrowing capacity at the banks.

It should also be noted in passing that the major
sales of Curtis magazines (as in the case with most
magazines) were sold pursuant to subscriptions, whereby the consumer paid a sum of money which entitled
him to receive copies of the magazine over a specified
period of time. Normally, so long as a magazine is
printed and distributed, these subscriptions are ful-
filled by delivery of the magazine. It is obvious,
however, that if the publication of a magazine is
terminated, either because of liquidation of the publisher or by determination of its management, the
subscribers have a clear contract right to recover the
unfulfilled portions of their subscriptions. Accordingly, each subscription might be considered to be
a liability, diminishing in amount as the magazine
is delivered. If the books of Curtis were kept in accordance with this suggestion, there would have been a
subscribers' liability at the end of 1967 which has been

estimated at about $90,000,000. However, no magazine
ever carries these subscriptions as a complete liability
or reserves a sufficient amount to pay them, and the
first class accounting firms who act for all of the large
circulation magazines approve the practice of not
including such subscription liabilities in the Balance
Sheet. Nevertheless, if a magazine publisher determines
or is forced to liquidate or decides to stop publication
of a magazine, such liabilities become a factor of
real importance.

A class action to recover such liabilities would
seem possible and I am informed that the Attorney-
General of the State of Massachusetts has actually
initiated such an action in respect of the local subscribers to the Saturday Evening Post.

Therefore, it would seem that in April, 1968
Curtis was probably insolvent in the equity sense in
that it was then unable to pay its debts as they matured
and, upon an economic reappraisal of its assets and
liabilities, might well have been insolvent in the bankruptcy sense, in that its assets at fair market value
may have been less than its liabilities.

In any event, it would seem certain that Curtis
was in deep trouble and that drastic measures were

essential. I suggest that this background is important
in viewing transactions which lie at the base of the
allegations of the Complaint and their probable merits.

## 2. The Bok Complaint

The action is pending in the United States District
Court for the Eastern District of Pennsylvania. It is
derivative and seeks recoveries for and in the right of
Curtis.

The complaint alleges:

(i) that on or about April 22, 1968 Messrs.
Martin Ackerman and E. Eugene Mason were elected
to the Board of Directors of Curtis and Mr. Ackerman
was elected President and Mr. Mason Secretary of the
Company; that Ackerman was the President of Perfect
and that Mason was an attorney who had acted for
him and that, therefore, Ackerman and Mason thereafter were under the disability of having conflicting
interests and acted in connection with the transactions
hereinafter outlined both for Curtis and Perfect; that
on or about June 29, 1968 Ackerman caused Curtis
and Perfect to enter into a contract pursuant to which
Curtis sold to Perfect the stock of Moore-Cottrell Subscription Agencies, Inc. and the assets of Keystone
Reader's Service, Inc. and Curtis Circulation Company

(the Circulation Companies) at a price of $12,500,000
in 5% notes of Perfect; that the transaction was unfair and fraudulent as to Curtis because in 1967 the
Circulation Companies had realized a pre-tax income
of approximately $3,700,000 and, therefore, their fair
value was substantially in excess of $12,500,000; that
Ackerman caused the contract of sale also to provide
that Curtis would warrant the collectability of all
accounts receivable transferred to Perfect as assets of
the Circulation Companies and to guarantee that the
Circulation Companies would produce a pre-tax
income of not less than $2,000,000 in each of the
ten years following the execution of the agreement;
that in order to give a semblance of fair dealing to
these transactions, the contract had provided and
Ackerman caused Curtis to retain Standard Research
Consultants, Inc. (Standard) to determine the fair
value of the Circulation Companies transferred as
above set forth, but furnished to Standard false
information designed to insure that Standard would
report a low valuation for the Circulation Companies;
and that shortly thereafter Ackerman and Perfect
caused Curtis to return to Perfect the $12,500,000
of convertible notes in exchange for $12,500,000
face value of accounts receivable of the Circulation
Companies which had been transferred to Perfect and
which were not worth $12,500,000.

(ii) That Curtis had certain bank loans consolidated
into a loan agreement with the First National Bank of
Boston (Bank Agreement); that the Bank Agreement
provided for foreclosure upon all of Curtis' assets in
the event of default; that Ackerman caused Perfect to
acquire said bank loans so as to substitute itself as the
lender possessed of all rights of the banks under the
Bank Agreement; that on October 14, 1968 Ackerman
caused Perfect to demand immediate payment of the
total bank loans, which were in excess of $13,000,000;
that Ackerman, acting for Curtis stated Curtis' inability to pay and then, acting for Perfect, caused Perfect
to "foreclose" on certain assets of Curtis; that, acting
for both Curtis and Perfect, Ackerman caused the
parties, rather than proceed through a formal foreclosure proceeding, to enter into an agreement (Foreclosure Agreement) whereby Curtis transferred to
Perfect the Saturday Evening Post, Holiday, Status
and Jack & Jill, without assuming any of the liabilities in connection with such publications, and that the
value of such assets was substantially in excess of the
bank debt to the knowledge of Ackerman and
Perfect.

(iii) That about August 14, 1968, Ackerman
informed the Board that the Ladies Home Journal,
California Home and American Home were operating
at a loss; that in reliance upon such information, the

Board of Directors was induced to enter into a contract with Downe Communications, Inc. (Downe), whereby these magazines were sold to Downe for 100,000 shares of Downe's stock represented to be worth $5,000,000; that the aforesaid representations to the Board were false and untrue to the knowledge of Ackerman because Curtis' accountants, Touche, Ross, Bailey & Smart (Touche) had certified a product line estimate showing that the Ladies Home Journal alone was earning at the rate of $1,600,000 per annum and that Ackerman then caused Curtis to sell the Downe shares to Perfect for $4,000,000 which was credited to Curtis under the Bank Agreement.

(iv) That about November 1, 1968, Ackerman and Perfect caused Curtis to incorporate a corporation known as Sepco; that they then caused Sepco to enter into a management contract with Perfect at a rate of $200,000 per annum; that about November 12, 1968, Ackerman caused Curtis to purchase 100,000 shares of Sepco for $5,000,000 in cash and Perfect to transfer the Saturday Evening Post, Holiday and Status to Sepco for the same number of shares; that the $5,000,000 contributed by Curtis to Sepco was substantially greater than the contribution by Perfect for the magazines contributed; and that thereafter Ackerman caused Curtis to absorb certain expenses and operating losses of Sepco without any consideration whatever.

(v) That Ackerman caused Curtis to transfer
certain surplus cash in the Pension Plan and Trust for
its employees to Perfect without any consideration
whatever and caused Curtis to indemnify Messrs. Ackerman, Mason and McCombs, who had been elected
Trustees of the Pension Plan, against any claims for
wrongful conduct in connection with the disposition
of such trust assets.

## 3. The Facts

The undersigned has conferred with Messrs.
Kalodner and Ackerman, as well as with counsel for
the various parties, and has reviewed most of the docu-
ments involved, including the exhibits annexed to the
complaint and the accounting material recently supplied to Curtis or Mr. Ackerman by Touche.

### (a) The Sale of the Circulation Companies and the "Foreclosure".

### (i)

It must be borne in mind that at the end of
January, 1968, the indebtedness of Curtis and its subsidiaries to the banks was approximately $13,000,000
and that all of the assets of Curtis had been pledged. It
is also quite clear that Curtis was in default in respect

of certain provisions of the Bank Agreement requiring
the maintenance of current assets, etc., so that the
banks were in a position, had they been so minded, to
demand immediate payment and that it would have
been obviously impossible for Curtis to meet such
demand.

Of course, a person may properly act as an agent
for both parties to a transaction, provided there is full
disclosure to both. However, when Mr. Ackerman
became President of Curtis, he placed himself in a most
difficult position in respect of dealings between Perfect
and Curtis. Indeed, it is suggested that no man, however honest and able, can negotiate a proper contract
with himself or between two principals for whom he
is acting as agent. In the dealings between Curtis and
Perfect, Mr. Ackerman, therefore, was in the unfortu-
nate position of being forced to be constantly mind-
ful of the best interests of the stockholders of both
Curtis and Perfect.

On the other hand, it must be remembered that
the Board of Curtis numbered 15 when the various
transactions hereinafter mentioned were consummated;
that 13 of such Directors had been on the Board
before Mr. Ackerman and Mr. Mason became members
of that Board and that each of the transactions was

placed before the Board and directed or ratified by it
and that, in every case, when such action took place,
the overwhelming majority of the Directors present
were "old" Directors.

(ii)

On June 27, 1968 Curtis sold the Circulation
Companies to Perfect, as alleged, for $12,500,000 in
Perfect's unregistered 5% Convertible Subordinated
notes due 1988. At the time of such sale, according to
Touche, the combined balance sheets of the Circulation
Companies indicated a net worth of $9,403,536.
Under date of March 17, 1969, Touche rendered a
report on certain transactions to Mr. Ackerman, who
was kind enough to furnish me with a copy. Exhibit
A hereto is a combined balance sheet of the Circulation
Companies as at May 19, 1968*.

The claim by plaintiffs that this transaction was
unfair is primarily based upon a statement alleged to
have been contained in a proof of a Registration
Statement filed by Perfect with the SEC (which never
became effective, largely because the earnings of the
Circulation Companies could not be verified by the
accountants) that the pre-tax earnings of the

---

*Although Touche has been accountants for Perfect, I am willing
to assume the accuracy of their figures.

Circulation Companies for 1967 had been $3,700,000
and, therefore, the indicated value of the Circulation
Companies was substantially in excess of $12,500,000.
But, the actual statement in the proof Registration
Statement was "Pro Forma Statement of income
before interest, corporate administrative expenses and
Federal and State income taxes $3,700,000". The
proper share of corporate administrative expenses and
interest has not been determined authoritatively by
the accountants. However, it is obviously substantial.
Moreover, Touche, in a special study which was before
the Board, indicated such pre-tax income as approximately $873,000 and the Income Tax Return for
the year 1967 indicated that such pre-tax income had
been approximately $1,163,000. Apparently, at the
time of the sale, the parties presumed that the proper
pre-tax income for 1967 of the Circulation Companies
had been in the neighborhood of $2,000,000, which
would normally leave an after-tax income of slightly
less than $1,000,000. This is evidenced by the fact
that the contract of June 27 contained a guarantee
by Curtis (Article V, paragraph B), which we discuss
later, that the pre-tax earnings during the ensuing ten
years would be not less than $2,000,000 per annum
and if they fell below that figure, Curtis would make
up the difference. There is also indication that there
was discussion of a capitalization rate of 12½% which,

applied to $1,000,000 of after-tax income, would
produce the tentative value of $12,500,000.

It would, therefore, seem quite clear that whatever were the actual pre-tax earnings of the Circulation
Companies for the year 1967, after application of a
proper share of general overhead and corporate expense,
they did not approximate $3,700,000.

In any event, the contract contains provision that
the $12,500,000 in notes is merely a tentative price
and that the ultimate and actual price to be paid by
Perfect is to be determined by Standard. Accordingly,
it is difficult to see how the original sale can be
attacked on the ground of inadequacy, since the price
has not as yet been determined.

Apparently, no one challenges the integrity or
disinterestedness of Standard. The complaint, however,
suggests that Mr. Ackerman gave Standard false information in a letter dated December 31, 1968, which is
annexed to the complaint as Exhibit B, in order to
induce Standard to report an improperly low value
for the Circulation Companies.

It should first be noted that a copy of this
letter was sent to the Board of Directors of Curtis.

Actually, however, the letter merely states that the
"shaky" financial condition of Curtis and delay by the
Circulation Companies in meeting their obligations
forced Perfect to guarantee such obligations and that
the general situation worried customers of the Circulation Companies. The letter also criticized the morale
of the employees of the Circulation Companies and
the operation of the computer services. So far as
statistics are concerned, the letter refers Standard to
Touche.

I cannot believe that this letter could have any
substantial effect on the evaluation produced by an
able and independent agency such as Standard. Moreover, if any of the statements were so greatly
incorrect as to be likely to influence the valuation
by Standard, any member of the Board could have
replied and, at this writing, I have assumed the
integrity of Touche and the reliability of the figures
proposed by it.

Accordingly, I suggest that it is unlikely that
there can or will be any substantial recovery by any
of the plaintiffs on the basis that the original sale
by Curtis to Perfect of the Circulation Companies
was fraudulent and for an inadequate price. Indeed,
I repeat, the price has not yet been determined and,

when it is, it can be attacked only by asserting that
Standard acted improperly or did not use accepted
methods of valuation.

(iii)

On the other hand, I do not believe that, in any
arms-length negotiation between a buyer and a seller
of a going business which had been operated by the
seller for many years, such seller would guarantee
maintenance of earnings for a period of ten years thereafter under operation by the buyer. To guarantee continued minimum income for a period of ten years of
a business which is subject to the usual economic
vicissitudes would seem rash; to give such a guarantee
under operation by somebody else would seem almost
foolhardy. While the exigencies of the then situation
required fast improvisation by Mr. Ackerman to save
Curtis, such exigencies also gave Mr. Ackerman, if he
desired to use them as a weapon, an added advantage
in pressuring Curtis into agreement with his proposals.
Pursuant to the terms of the agreement, this guarantee
continues to subsist and bind Curtis. Accordingly,
while I believe that Mr. Ackerman, having the interests
of the Perfect stockholders in mind, acted honestly
and was guilty of no fraud, nevertheless, I consider
this guarantee to be unfair to Curtis and I strongly
recommend that this Committee or the Board use

its best interests to secure a cancellation by Perfect of
this guarantee.

(iv)

On August 5, 1968, the $12,500,000 of Perfect
notes were returned to Perfect and Perfect returned to
Curtis $12,500,000 of accounts receivable of the
Circulation Companies. It has been suggested that
there were two added steps in this transaction, i.e.,
that Perfect purchased the notes for $12,500,000 in
cash and that Curtis purchased the accounts receivable
for such $12,500,000 in cash. However, whether any
actual cash was passed or not, the transaction washes
out and the effect is that Perfect repossessed itself of
its own notes and Curtis repossessed the accounts
receivable. In its report of March 17, 1968, Touche
analyzes this transaction, together with further
advances of $2,850,000 by Perfect under the Bank
Agreement. A copy of such analysis is Exhibit B
hereto.

On its face, this transaction would seem to be
subject, to a lesser degree, to the same criticism
which is above leveled at the guarantee of income.
Plaintiffs would seem justified in attacking it. Standing alone, the guarantee by Curtis of its accounts
receivable and the action by Perfect in forcing Curtis

to take back less than all of the assets of the Circulation Companies for the entire consideration received
for them would seem of dubious propriety. However,
whether there was any actual fraud by Perfect and
Mr. Ackerman or damage to Curtis depends upon the
effect of a series of subsequent transactions.

(v)

Thereafter, and on October 14, 1968 (Exhibit
D annexed to the Bok complaint), Perfect proceeded
with the so-called "foreclosure". There is no question
about Curtis' default under the Bank Agreement.
Perfect had by now acquired all of the bank debt and
was subrogated to all rights of the banks. Nevertheless,
it is clear that Mr. Ackerman's concern for Perfect
and its stockholders, rather than his concern for
Curtis and its stockholders, dictated the procedure.
The position of double representation continues to
present problems.

Exhibit C hereto is Touche's analysis of all other
transactions between Curtis and Perfect prior to October
14, 1968. It shows a balance of $11,604,000 due on that
date from Curtis to Perfect, virtually all of which represented direct loans by the banks and Perfect, reduced
by a credit for the sale of certain magazines to Downe—
which transaction is discussed later.

Pursuant to the Foreclosure Agreement, Curtis transferred to Perfect the Saturday Evening Post, Holiday, Status and Jack & Jill, and Perfect repossessed itself of the same accounts receivable which it had returned to Curtis when it reacquired the $12,500,000 of its notes, diminished by payments received by Curtis after August 5, 1968. Moreover, it reacquired such accounts receivable at face value, against debt, which cannot be questioned. The Foreclosure Agreement recites that the assets taken by Perfect have a value "equivalent" to all indebtedness by Curtis to Perfect or the banks, and the assets transferred thereunder are accepted by Perfect in full "satisfaction" of all obligations by Curtis to Perfect. Thus, on October 14, 1968, Curtis had fully paid the banks and Perfect. The analysis by Touche of this "foreclosure" is Exhibit D hereto.

It will first be noted that this transaction, fair or not in other respects, would seem to wash out any claims arising from the original sale of the Circulation Companies to Curtis or the August 5th transactions. Since Curtis originally transferred these assets at face value and Perfect took them back at face value, there would seem to be no room for controversy concerning them.

No one has made any real attempt to value any of the four magazines transferred under the Foreclosure Agreement. Touche has made "product line" studies of income which show estimated annualized results for 1968, before allocation of any of about $17,000,000 of general overhead, as follows:

| Saturday Evening Post | Holiday | Jack & Jill |
|---|---|---|
| (1,324) | (181) | (314) |

No figures have been seen for Status.

Moreover, as we shall see, all of these magazines, except Jack & Jill, ended up in Sepco. We reserve further discussions of their values for our discussion of the Sepco transaction.

Nevertheless, it should be noted that Exhibit C indicates a total debt by Curtis to Perfect on October 14, 1968 of $11,604,000, whereas Exhibit D reflects assets (excluding the four magazines) received by Perfect under the Foreclosure Agreement, having a book value of $13,500,000—thus indicating receipt by Perfect of excess assets (giving no values to the four magazines), at book values of $1,896,000.

However, even yet no conclusions are possible until subsequent transactions are considered.

(vi)

Exhibit E hereto constitutes an analysis by Touche
of all transactions between Curtis and Perfect from
October 14, 1968 to December 31, 1968 and, so far
as we know, there were no transactions between Curtis
and Perfect in 1969. Since Touche's statement opens
with the balance of $11,604,000 from Exhibit C, it
purports to be a complete analysis (except for any
values inhering in the Circulation Companies beyond
the accounts receivable or the four magazines transferred under the Foreclosure Agreement). After all
transactions between Curtis and Perfect, it will be
noted that Touche comes up with an overall balance
due from Curtis to Perfect as at December 31, 1968
of $4,495,000. In this connection it should be noted
that this amount is really only an amount which Perfect is entitled to retain out of Curtis' assets in its
hands, not a presently collectible debt because the
assets transferred under the Foreclosure Agreement
were accepted by Perfect "in full satisfaction" of
Curtis' obligations to it.

We return to this matter under our discussion
infra of the Sepco transaction.

4. The Sale of Ladies Home Journal, American Home
   and California Home to Downe.

This transaction is simple. Curtis sold the above magazines to Downe for 100,000 shares of Downe's common stock. Downe, unlike Perfect in the purchase of the Circulation Companies and the Foreclosure Agreement, assumed substantially all liabilities of the magazines, including unfulfilled subscriptions. The shares were delivered to Perfect, which sold them for $4,472,000 and gave Curtis credit for that amount against its obligations under the Bank Agreement (see Exhibit C hereto).

Thus, the only basis for any claim is that the price of the magazines was wholly inadequate and known by Ackerman and Downe to be inadequate. I do not believe that this claim can be sustained.

The complaint refers to a "conspiracy" and a pro forma study by Touche, which projected annual earnings of $1,600,000 for the Journal alone, but again that was an hypothetical projection before allocation of any share of the $17,000,000 of general overhead and the actual figures indicate losses as follows:

| 1966 | 1965 | 1964 | 1963 |
|------|------|------|------|
| $1,001,000 | $1,247,000 | $755,000 | $247,000 |

So far as I have been able to ascertain, neither Mr. Ackerman nor Perfect has any interest in Downe. Hence, I can find no evidence of conspiracy and I believe this claim to be without merit.

## 5. The Sepco Transaction

Shortly after the "foreclosure", the parties organized Sepco. Curtis purchased 50% of its shares for $5,000,000 cash, which it withdrew from the Pension Fund; Perfect transferred the Saturday Evening Post, Holiday and Status (retaining Jack & Jill), which it had acquired under the Foreclosure Agreement for the remaining 50% of Sepco's stock. Sepco also immediately entered into a Management Agreement with Perfect, calling for approximately $200,000 annual management fees to Perfect and Mr. Ackerman became President of Sepco.

If the transactions had stopped here, a serious question would be raised as to whether the three magazines were worth $5,000,000, so that Perfect paid as much for its 50% of Sepco's stock as did Curtis and, in any event, there is a question as to the fairness of and need for the Management Contract.

However, on November 11, 1968, the parties entered into an agreement which, in effect, returned

to Curtis its right of redemption of the assets possessed
by Perfect under the Foreclosure Agreement and, in
substance, provided that when, as and if Perfect
received full payment of its indebtedness (plus any
expenses) from the accounts receivable of the Circulation Companies and/or Jack & Jill, it would transfer
its stock in Sepco to Curtis, together with any remaining assets and, of course, Curtis would have satisfied
all of its obligations to Perfect.

As we have seen, as at December 31, 1968, the
balance owed by Curtis to Perfect, according to Touche,
was $4,495,000.

Perhaps it should be observed that Perfect is
under no obligation to sell Jack & Jill and that the
remaining accounts receivable may be expected to be
the most difficult of collection. However, the remaining accounts receivable total approximately $7,000,000
and Jack & Jill unquestionably has value. In any event,
if the accounts receivable, or the accounts receivable
together with the proceeds of any sale by Perfect of
Jack & Jill, equal $4,495,000, Perfect will be obligated
to transfer its Sepco stock to Curtis, so that Curtis
will then own 100% of Sepco. Perfect will also be
obligated to return to Curtis any remaining uncollected
accounts receivable and, if not sold, Jack & Jill.

Indeed, if Curtis preferred and could raise the money, it could pay Perfect the $4,495,000, plus any accrued expenses and interest, and secure a return of all assets acquired by Perfect under the Foreclosure Agreement.

## 6. Pension Plan Funds

Obviously, if Perfect took and retained any cash from the Pension Fund, without applying it to Curtis' debt, there is a claim. However, I have found no evidence that such is the case.

## 7. Conclusions

There may be minor unmentioned matters which are still open between Curtis and Perfect. However, no one questions the validity of the debt owed by Curtis to Perfect under the Bank Agreement. All of it represents actual advances to Curtis or payment of admitted obligations of Curtis. Despite the complicated and manifold intercompany transactions between Curtis and Perfect, in respect of which Mr. Ackerman acted for both parties, the upshot seems to be (a) that the apparent remaining "indebtedness" of $4,495,000 must be increased or decreased, depending upon whether Standard appraises the value of the Circulation Companies as at the time of transfer below or above $12,500,000; and (b) no Curtis assets will be retained by Perfect other than those disposed of, the proceeds of which were credited against the Curtis debt.

Accordingly, I cannot find any evidence of fraud or overreaching and conclude that no substantial recovery for Curtis can result from a prosecution of the Bok action.

On the other hand, as indicated above, I think that the guarantee by Curtis of the pre-tax income of the Circulation Companies is neither fair nor appropriate. I can understand its inclusion at the outset, but even then, the time period was far too long. Perfect now has acquired the "feel" of the operation of the Circulation Companies. In my opinion, the guarantee of earnings should be cancelled and terminated.

Also, although I have no record of hours put in or by whom, it is my belief that the $200,000 Management Agreement should be substantially modified. Indeed, I suggest that since Curtis may ultimately expect to repossess Sepco in the near future, that arrangements be made to make the management of Curtis a full partner with the management of Perfect in the operation of Sepco and that any fees to come off the top of Sepco's earnings be equalized.

I also suggest that perhaps an evaluation could be made or agreed upon of Jack & Jill. Maybe it has sufficient value so that retention by Perfect would liquidate the remaining obligations of Curtis.

Finally, I am strongly of the opinion that the Bok action, as well as the Kalodner and Tait cases, should be promptly disposed of. In my view, prosecution of these cases, in the blaze of publicity which cannot be avoided, is now doing and will continue to do vastly more harm to Curtis, Perfect and Sepco than can ever be recovered for Curtis at the end of the road.

Very truly yours,

SP:pk

## IN THE UNITED STATES DISTRICT COURT
## FOR THE EASTERN DISTRICT OF PENNSYLVANIA

| | |
|---|---|
| CARY W. BOK | **CIVIL ACTION** |
| v. | **NO. 69-305** |
| MARTIN S. ACKERMAN, et al. | |

## NOTICE OF HEARING ON PROPOSED SETTLEMENT OF CLAIMS AMONG THE CURTIS PUBLISHING COMPANY, PERFECT FILM & CHEMICAL CORPORATION, THE SATURDAY EVENING POST COMPANY, MARTIN S. ACKERMAN, E. EUGENE MASON, MILTON S. GOULD, G. B. McCOMBS AND CERTAIN OTHERS.

TO ALL SHAREHOLDERS OF THE CURTIS PUBLISHING COMPANY:

NOTICE IS HEREBY GIVEN that a hearing will be held at 10 A.M. on January 21, 1970 in the United States Court House, 9th and Chestnut Streets, Philadelphia, Pennsylvania, 19107 before The Honorable A. Leon Higginbotham, District Court Judge, for the purpose of approving a settlement of all claims of The Curtis Publishing Company ("Curtis") and The Saturday Evening Post Company ("Sepco") against Perfect Film & Chemical Corporation ("Perfect"), Martin S. Ackerman, E. Eugene Mason, Milton S. Gould, G. B. McCombs and the present and/or former officers, directors and alleged controlling shareholders of Curtis and of all claims of Perfect against Curtis and Sepco. At that time you may appear and be heard, in person or through counsel, with respect to the proposed settlement.

The terms of the proposed settlement are as follows:

1. Curtis will become the owner of all of the capital stock of Sepco free of all liens and contract rights presently asserted by Perfect.

2. Perfect will transfer to Sepco all copyrights, trademarks, assets and all of its right and title to Jack & Jill Magazine.

3. Perfect will release or record all liens and relinquish all rights presently asserted by it relating to Holiday Magazine, Status Magazine, The Saturday Evening Post Magazine and all other assets and property of Curtis, Sepco and any subsidiary of Curtis.

4. All assets and property of Curtis and any subsidiary thereof acquired by Perfect in lieu of fore-closure by agreement dated October 14, 1968 (other than property converted to cash and credited to Curtis' account) shall be returned to Curtis.

5. Perfect will retain the Circulation and Subscription Companies and other assets transferred to Perfect by Curtis by agreement dated June 29, 1968. In lieu of the determination of consideration by Standard Research Consultants, Inc. contemplated in the said agreement, the fair and equitable price as of June 29, 1968, of the assets transferred under the said agreement and the credit, if any, to be given Perfect for previous payments to Curtis will be determined finally by a panel of arbitrators to be appointed as follows:

Curtis and Perfect shall each select one arbitrator and the two arbitrators so selected will select a third, or, if they are unable to agree, the third arbitrator will be selected according to the method provided by the American Arbitration Association.

6. The balance, if any, determined by such arbitration to be remaining to be paid on account of the June 29, 1968 agreement will be paid in installments at the rate of $300,000 per year with all payments due to be made in five years. This method of payment replaces the provisions in the contract which provided for payment in the form of long-term notes.

7. Perfect will purchase from Curtis the accounts receivable from regional subscription sales franchise holders representing Curtis Circulation Company notes receivable at a price of approximately $395,000.

8. Balances due between Curtis and Perfect under The Basic Bank Agreement and intercompany accounts (including the purchase by Perfect of accounts receivable as described in Paragraph 7) between Curtis and Perfect will be paid. In addition, Perfect will pay a special credit of $350,000, to Curtis. In the event that Curtis, Perfect and their respective accountants shall not have reached agreement as to such balances due on or before January 31, 1970, the matter will be submitted to arbitration in the manner described in Paragraph 5.

9. For a period of two years or the period of publication, whichever is shorter, the Circulation and Subscription Companies acquired by Perfect shall have exclusive representation of Holiday, Jack & Jill, and Status Magazines in all subscription and single-copy sales with the exception of direct mail subscription solicitation performed by Sepco, Curtis or any of the respective magazines at rates and services which are competitive to that provided by competitors.

10. The following actions involving disputes between the parties will be dismissed with prejudice:

*Cary W. Bok v. Martin S. Ackerman, et al.,* U.S.D.C.S.D. of Pa., Civil Action No. 69-305

*The Curtis Publishing Company v. Perfect Film & Chemical Corporation,* U.S.D.C.E.D. of Pa. Civil Action No. 69-817

*Miriam J. Wolf v. Martin S. Ackerman, et al.,* U.S.D.C.S.D. of N.Y., Civil Action No. 69 Civ. 771 (transferred to U.S.D.C.E.D. of Pa.)

*Philip P. Kalodner v. The Curtis Publishing Company et al.,* Philadelphia Court of Common Pleas, February Term, 1969, No. 192

*Frank M. Tait v. Cary W. Bok,* Supreme Court of New York, No. 08025-1969

and releases will be exchanged among the parties to all of these actions and among former directors of the corporate parties. Under the proposed settlement, all claims of the classes represented by plaintiffs in said suits will be finally terminated.

The proposed settlement agreement in full is filed of record as Exhibit A to Motion for Approval of Compromise Settlement in the above-captioned action and is available for your inspection at the office of the Clerk of the District Court, United States Court House, Philadelphia, Pennsylvania.

If you wish to object to the terms of the proposed Compromise Settlement, you are required to file a statement of the grounds therefor, in writing, with the Clerk of the Court, at the following address, no later than January 16, 1970.

John H. Harding, Esquire
Clerk of The United States District
   Court for the Eastern District of
   Pennsylvania
Post Office Box 989
Philadelphia, Pennsylvania 19105

NOTE:
Judge Higginbotham has entered Orders dismissing with prejudice both Bok v. Ackerman (69-305) and Wolf v. Ackerman (69-2879).